Snapshots from a Broken Camera

A Collection of Short Stories About my Life

Jeanne Barkemeijer de Wit

Published by

Jeanne and Johnnie Johnson / 1551 West Chateau Avenue/ Anaheim, CA 92802-1315

barkemeijer@gmail.com

Printed in the United States of America.

First Edition

WARNING: This book is intended for adults ONLY, and is not recommended for children.

Graphic Sexual Content. The contents of this book describes various forms of child abuse, including neglect, sexual, physical and emotional abuse.

If you are a survivor of child abuse, and/or are currently diagnosed as having M.P.D., D.I.D., or P.T.S.D., the contents of this book may trigger flashbacks and/or dissociative episodes. Before reading this book, make sure you are in a safe place.

❧Dedications❧

Melvin C. Johnson
Friend, Mentor & Second Dad

Thank you for allowing me to be a part of your family
and for showing me what unconditional love is.

F. Michael Trevitt, PhD
Friend, Teacher & Guide

Thank you for your compassionate care and guidance.

You are both sorely missed

Mary J. Chambers, L.C.S.W
Voice of Compassion & Understanding

For everything you are and everything you do
I Thank You

❧Acknowledgments❧

To all who have helped heal my mind body and soul

Chun Kee Ryu, MD
Mary White, MD
Trula Michaels De La Calle, MD
Walter K. Heuler, MD
J.H. Rick Massimino, MD
Carol Montsinger
Vicky Zinser
Donna Constantine, RN
Dorothy V. Calabrese, MD
Cameron Charles Switzer

My Kaiser Permanente Physicians

Johnson Murray, MD
Pranav Vinykant Shah, MD
Kumarapuram V. Venkatasubramaniam, MD
Benjamin Spurgeon, D.O.
Thomas Ducmy Nguyen, D.O.

Table of Contents

Forward

I started writing this book in 1991, a year or so after my Dad died. Life was brutally hard back then. Mom was still suffering from the effects of her stroke. For a while I tried holding on to my job while also caring for my Mom (read the book). My physical health nose dived and I crashed and burned. I've been struggling to regain my health ever since. (Multiple small strokes and a pulmonary embolism later, I'm still chugging along hoping for the best.)

F. Michael Trevitt, PhD (my therapist in 1991) suggested I write everything down, more for myself than anyone else. So I journaled and wrote a couple of newspaper articles on life with Multiple Personality Disorder. I was surprised at how popular my stories were.

People who knew I had MPD (I didn't keep it secret back in the day) would ask me what it was like to be a multiple, what it felt like to "Switch", and all sorts of invasive and private questions. Invariably, some idiot asked me to go in great detail about the sexual abuse. Then I'd stress and vanish into some dark place within myself.

A lot of people's questions stressed the hell out of me, so much so I ended up losing time and other personalities would step in and take over. I was taking care of my still abusive Mom and trying to get my head straight. I didn't understand people's fascination with my pain. (Still don't) I half joked to the doctor that I felt as if I were writing psychological porn. Mostly I worried about people's reasons for needing to know so much about the sexual details of my life.

Every time I got close to finishing I either burned what I'd written or toss my pages in the trash. When I started writing by computer, I'd only get so far before I deleted everything I'd written from the computer.

So here I am 22 years and almost 100,000 words later, wondering about the reasons I started writing this in the first place, and still worrying about what people will think of me after they read it.

There's a part of me which aches to leave the past behind. But so far I haven't been able to do that. Just when I think I'm clear of the pain that memories bring, I'll hear a song, or the sky turns the same color as the day I was raped, and suddenly I'm flooded with memories so real they take my breath away.

Remembering wouldn't be so bad if the memories didn't feel so God damned real. It's as if I'm stuck inside a broken time machine, one moment I'm living in real time, the next I'm lost somewhere long ago. When I return, I'm forced to remember that everyone I loved is dead.

I have a new therapist now, Mary Chambers, who believes my story will help survivors like myself. I cried the day she told me that. The idea that some other child was forced to endure the things I had, is almost more than I can comprehend. The idea that my journey to find a life beyond all the pain could help someone else propels me forward. As of today I've finished nearly 50,000 words with every intention of publishing.

In my humble opinion, "Adult Survivor" is a deeply personal and extremely subjective term. Every day I fight to survive my past, suicide is ALWAYS in the back of my mind. While I used to believe otherwise, the truth is there are NO survivors of child abuse. Anyone who tells you otherwise is delusional or has been grossly misinformed. The best you can hope for is to grow beyond the pain.

I am more than my past, and hopefully stronger than the pain that comes with my memories. I long for grace, pray for salvation, and hope peace eventually finds its way into my soul. I thank God I beat the statistical odds and didn't become a carbon copy of my abusers. God willing my body will heal, along with my heart, soul and mind.

Jeanne Barkemeijer de Wit
Anaheim, CA

September 2013

∽Introduction

Each chapter of this book was written as a story within itself, a snapshot if you will, of different periods in my life. Hence the name of the title. If you look closely you'll notice grammatical errors, errors in syntax and more. There's a reason for these inconsistencies. The stories are written by my various alters.

My sister alters range in age from infancy into my 50s and ages in between. Some of our views on life, and the things they [we] have experienced, differ. My sisters speak to me through the narrator. My job is to sit back and type what they tell me.

I've been listening to the narrator talking to me for most of my life. The narrator has always helped me keep focus on life events. She allows me a way of seeing, hearing, and feeling, what my other parts are experiencing without losing my grip on reality.

Feel free to start reading from ANY chapter, as nothing has been written in sequence. If a story wanders a bit when you read it, realize you are reading thoughts as they flow forward from my brain.

Remembering has NEVER been" easy, and writing this book has been one of the most difficult projects I have ever taken on.

⌒Biography

Jeanne Barkemeijer de Wit is the first American born member of her family. The rest of her family, including her brother Dick, were all born in the Netherlands. Her parents were Nel and Dick Barkemeijer de Wit.

Jeanne lives with her husband Johnnie in Anaheim, California. They have both been active in Greyhound rescue for decades, and share their home with two retired Greyhound racers (Harvey and Raleigh) and a Borador (Pupper) they rescued from the pound.

Jeanne's family was adopted by three cats, (Verbal, a 26 year old Calico), (Tanja, a 4 year old Siamese) and (Mookie, a 2 year old Bengal Mix with developmental issues) who run the entire household (including the dogs).

Jeanne has been on Social Security Disability since around 1990. As of 2013, she was still undergoing therapy for mental health issues. She still loses time and dissociates. In September 2013, when this book was first published, she was also recovering from a pulmonary embolism and multiple small strokes.

"Snapshots from a Broken Camera", an autobiography based on her life and the abuse she suffered. This work is Jeanne's first book.

Jeanne's biographical information has been listed in the following since 1990:
Marquis Who's Who in America [Macmillan Directory Division]
Marquis Who's Who in American Women [Macmillan Directory Division]
Marquis Who's Who in the World [Macmillan Directory Division]

Jeanne is also a published composer / musician, who's music CDs can be listened to and/or purchased online. Additionally Jeanne's illustrations, paintings, graphics, photography and other stories, have been displayed and/or published internationally and garnered her numerous awards.

✍I Want to go Home

I want to go home.

Few people have any idea how gut wrenching a statement this is for me ... or why.

The home I live in and now call my own, originally belonged to my husband's father. Long story that. While I'm grateful to have a home, this one still doesn't quite feel like mine.

I live surrounded by Johnson family ghosts. Loving Ghosts of countless birthdays, holidays, illness, sorrow, joy, family meals and gatherings. Ghosts residing deep inside fragrant cedar scented drawers and closets ... and sheltered within countless boxes. All containing photos, letters and more ... memories intermingled with dust and tears.

I want to go home ... to my childhood home ... a world I fight to remember and struggle to forget.

Most days I reside in a sort of half life now, where past memories are past memories. Simple right? I wish. But, and here's the rub, memories ::: my memories ::: are always there. Some are just below the surface waiting to bob up. Some memories are buried too deep to see, but I can still feel them and react.

There are times when remembering is hard bitter work. Today's one of those days. Today I need to type as fast as I can. Before the fog slithers back into my brain and I forget. Before the memories fade from my mind. Before the colors and the streets and the smells vanish, and I'm left standing alone in the dark.

I want to go home ...

I remember Santa Ana ... Bristol street a few blocks from my home ... I would walk up and down that street for hours on end ... a little kid, taking in the sights and smells ... the A and P on the corner of Bristol and McFadden ... the Carnation Ice Cream parlor, Bob's Owl Rexall, their big picture window, lined with impossibly large glass apothecary jars filled with brightly colored water, Me n Ed's Pizza ::: ye old Pizza Parlor ::: their ancient upright piano ::: ye old piano ::: the sign painted above the cigarette machine - reading "ye old coffin nails" Freddie's restaurant.

I want to go home ...

There was a Volkswagen dealership on the corner of Bristol and Edinger where a furniture store used to be ... now there's a strip mall. Matter Dai was located across the street ::: still is ::: sort'a kind'a catty cornered. I don't remember the exact year, 1963 I think, they built a Thrifty Drug across the street, where Dad would take me for nickel ice cream cones, and my folks would go for dinner when they built a restaurant inside. All you can eat specials of fish or chicken or liver ... too much food.

I remember the new air conditioned post office they built across the street from my school ... Diamond Elementary. I remember sitting in the car while parked in front of the post office on a brutally hot day. Waiting for my mother, the hot sun burning my skin, the 3pm sky as white as steam, so white that all the colors in the world melted away with the heat and the bright light until I melted with them and vanished.

I rode home a shadow, bones only, rattling in the car, my mother clueless to the fact I had gone, was gone, would never return. I watched glints of blue fade in and out between the wind and the sky and forgot who I was ... dizzy from the heat and the blinding white light.

I want to go home ...

I wish I could go home, to places I remember. To the In and Out on main street, the one selling hot oily melon sized bags of crisp salty dark brown fries. La Fonda's Mexican Restaurant, homemade tacos, corn chips, confetti salad with sugary dressing, Dr Pepper in bottles, my father talking with the owner, chewing gum cigars and candy cigarettes in my pocket on the way home. The wishing well in front, pennies in the water. The late evening sound of Main street with no cars. The color of the stars ... smell of a cool spring night ... and the warmth of my father's strong hand holding mine.

I want to go home ...

To my own bed, with the sound of my brother's 1000 aquariums gurgling from the next room ... my brother's room, the light from the hallway sneaking into my bedroom from under my door, the comforting sound of my father's shoes clomp clomp clomping on the hardwood floor, the television blaring in the distance, the high pitched squeak my bedroom door made when Dad opened it to check on me, hug me, kiss me and bid me goodnight. The acrid smell of cigarette tobacco, old spice and sweat ... Dad's smell, "Goodnight Shrimpy", Dad's name for me ... "Ik houd van jau" (I love you.) I love you to Papa. I always will ...

I want to go home ...

To Tony and Tanja and Pupper and Beaster and Junior. My four legged friends. Wiggly and soft and warm. So many days and nights ... they were there ... to comfort and love me. They were there when Mom went crazy, when I was sick, when ambulances came for Mom, when Steve (our gardener ... her lover) raped me, when Amy (my Grandmother) died and Mom began to hate me. They were there.

I want to go home .

I can never go home. Someone pulled me away. Away from my life ::: my parents ::: my family ::: my cats ::: my dogs ::: my bed and my home. Someone who choked me and left me to die alone on my bathroom floor, face down in the toilet. Someone who found me when I was home alone (my brother across the street) sick in bed. The man in the hallway, who haunts my dreams and always returns.

In dreams I see him standing in the doorway of my room. He stands in the doorway and looks at me in my bed. In dreams he returns over and over and over again. One minute he is at the door, the next he has my face in his hands and is pushing something I can't see deep within my throat ::: something wet hard and silky smooth ::: gagging me.

He told me he would kill me if I told my Mom. I'm barely 9, Defiant, scared, hurt and sick ... I told him I was telling my mother. "So there, go ahead and kill me." Terrified stupid child that I was I dared him to do his worst. "You can't make me NOT tell." His fingers on my throat, his eyes searing my skin, my breath gone, my soul gone, my life gone. He left me laying on the floor in a pool of vomit and something worse.

This after the bad thing in my mouth, choking me. The bad taste, the sticky fowl smelling awful thing that made me vomit all over the floor. He held my hair and face so I couldn't move. I was sick and he made me sicker. My throat hurt and he made it hurt more.

Don't tell ... don't tell. Stupidly defiant child, I screamed no! You can't make me! No help, no family, only pain. He choked me forever ... until I saw millions of flickering stars orbiting my face and my heart exploded inside my chest. He choked me until my warm safe world turned cold dark and ugly. He choked me until I died.

Sadly my death didn't last long. When I awoke, the blue walls of my room had turned white, as white as steam, whiter than any white the world had ever seen and melted me away to nothing and I was gone. The only living thing remaining in my room were the ugly blue red purple rings surrounding my neck.

The sound and feel and taste of that late spring afternoon are permanently etched upon my soul ::: buried deep within a dark cold place.

There are still times I fly into a wild panic ... for no reason. Suddenly I see his face ::: the man who raped me ::: and the outline of him standing in the doorway. I hear the sound of my brother across the street shooting hoops with Billy Wilkins. The thud his basket ball makes when hits the Wilkins' garage door.

Close enough to hear my brother's laughter. Close enough to hear his basketball thudding against the Wilkins' garage. Close enough to feel almost safe. So close and yet too far for help.

I can still hear the sound of my own screams echoing inside my scull, trying to escape my bruised and battered throat. I can still smell the scent of orange blossom from a thousand distant orange groves intermingled with the pungent odor of freshly cut and watered grass. The smell of gasoline on Steve's clothing and the smell of Lysol from the just cleaned bathroom floor still burns my eyes as I struggle to get away.

When it's over, and the man has gone, I hear the creaking of the hardwood floor as the wind sweeps beneath my home ... the sigh-whoosh sound of our central heating as the furnace cycles on. I'm safe, I'm home, all is well. I breathe again, as rain drops tick tick tick upon my bedroom window.

A familiar fog shrouds my brain, I'm safe, I'm home, all is well. I hear the musical gurgling of my bathroom toilet and I breathe deeper. Sounds familiar sounds safe ... calm me ... sounds of home. The past is dead. I'm safe, I'm home, all is well.

Snapshots from a Broken Camera

I want to go home.

I ache to go home … feel my own bed … run down the street with my greyhound Junior padding beside me … kiss my grandmother … hug my Dad … start over … forget … heal … recover everything that was stolen from me all those years ago. I want to go home.

The nine year old I once was resides within me and longs for family. She doesn't understand that I'm old and everyone I ever loved and cared about, who ever loved and cared for me … is dead.

I can never go home. Never. The finality of that simple statement floods me with grief. I fear I'll never be safe, know I can never go home and that all is definitely not well.

I want to go home

Remembering Happy Remembering Sad

I've been trying to remember happy times with my Mom and my family. Times when I didn't feel afraid, family members weren't sick or dying and home-life was peaceful. Mostly I can't, which makes me want to cry.

Why can't I remember? Is there something wrong with me? I don't understand.

I can remember bits of pieces, tiny moments in time when life felt normal, and I felt safe and warm and loved. But they always ended too quickly. Mom's moods could shift quickly and turn the world sideways.

"I see I see what you don't see and the color is ..." Mom loved playing games with us when we were little. I spy, hide and seek, sing along, story time. I don't think she liked us as much when we got older. I guess control was a big thing with her. The older we got, the harder she had to work to keep us the way she wanted us to be.

I can never remember an extended period when Mom was simply happy. I can't remember her singing to herself, laughing spontaneously at simple things, or looking happy for no reason. There was ALWAYS a reason for EVERYTHING Mom felt. I imagine life was exhausting for her.

Dad, on the other hand, was ALWAYS happy and silly and crude. He'd prance around the house making silly noises (he and I both have Tourettes) and whistling loudly. He called my flip flops "klote klappers", which is crude Amsterdam slang for nut crackers (if you get my drift).

By the time I was four, I was swearing like a Dutch dock worker. I didn't know what in the heck I was saying, I only knew my Dad used those words all the time. Words like klootzak and boerenlul, which sounded wonderfully hilarious to me as a child. There was one word, Godverdomme, (pronounced hot ver dome eh) which I'd NEVER say. Dad used it only when he was angry. The word scared me to death.

I'd tell you what the words mean, but the definitions are easily lost in translation. Suffice it to say that Amsterdamers like my Dad enjoyed commenting on people's physical short comings.

Snapshots from a Broken Camera

Belches and Farts and Other Rare Family Gifts

Dad loved to fart and burp, the louder the better, usually in public places. If I was standing next to him when he farted, he'd look me in the eye and loudly say "Jeanne, shame on you." Unfortunately Dad generally saved his farts for when he and I were walking down a busy isle in Kmart.

Dad also loved asking people to "pull his finger", at which point he'd fart on demand. Dad always made me laugh.

Mom laughed at movies were some poor guy gets kicked in the nuts. She seemed to take joy in watching men in pain. Scenes which made my Dad flinch or laugh uncomfortably, made Mom roar with laughter.

When Blazing Saddles came out, Michael (my first husband) and I took Mom and Dad to see it. Dad laughed all the way through the movie. There were a lot of pratfalls in the Movie so we assumed there was at least half a chance Mom would laugh to.

When the campfire scene came on, Mike and I both expected Dad to laugh. After all, farting was Dad's thing. Naturally Dad added his own farting noises during the movie. But we were all shocked into silence when my Mom started laughing so loud she could be heard outside the building.

The fact that Mom laughed through a good portion of Blazing Saddles surprised us all.

When the movie was over, and we were walking in the parking lot, Mike went and gave my Mom a hug. He told her he was glad she had liked the movie. "Excuse me?" My Mom said imperiously, looking at Mike like he was out of his mind. "What makes you think I like that kind of cheap crap?" Mike started laughing at my Mom, which was the wrong thing to do and set her off on a noisy tangent.

"Why did you buy me such a God damned big soda pop? Why did you fill it with ice? I HATE big cups! I hate icy cold soda pop. Just look at my wet hands, this cup is sweating all over me! And I hated this stupid movie!" To make her point, Mom threw the soda pop over her shoulder. The problem was, she hit some poor guy in white bell bottoms who was standing right behind her.

"Mrs. B!" said Mike "What was THAT all about? Don't you think you should stop and apologize?"

"Shut up Michael" whispered my Mom. "Keep walking, Keep walking!" She literally flew to our car. She never did stop to apologize. Everyone was laughing on the way home.

Bowel movements, shitting and farts and/or the process of shitting and farting seem to have been a running theme in my family. My maternal grandfather Opa purchased whoopee cushions to surprise guests. He was known for placing whoopee cushions under the seat of the most unsuspecting and straight-laced guest at his home. He also had fake shit, he enjoyed leaving in unusual places.

When my Aunt asked him to teach her how to say I love you to my Uncle in Dutch. He taught her to say "I love you my green green shitter." [Ik hou van je mijn groene groen pooper.]

Dinner with Piet

My family was friends with a Dutch contortionist named Piet Van Brecht. Piet performed all over the world, and had been on Ed Sullivan a number of times.

HOLD YOUR BREATH!

PIET VAN BRECHTS
FUN FROM HOLLAND

Piet was famous for folding his legs behind his neck, balancing on the end of a pool cue and then either ironing is pants or playing his clarinet. My parents loved inviting Piet and his family to our home. After dinner Piet would always perform.

The problem was, Mom always fixed enough food to feed any army. Food, in her mind, was love.

Piet had this tube thing, just big enough for him to crawl into (he was a skinny guy). He'd crawl in one end, fold himself in half and then crawl out the other end.

One night he must have eaten too much food, because half way though he got stuck. It took four men to pull him out of the tube.

Then Piet and all the guys started farting. They broke into heated debate as to how flammable farts were, and what the best way was to set them on fire.

Snapshots from a Broken Camera

The men in the house were moving our kitchen table, when Mom decided to quickly ushered me out of the kitchen, saying it was my bedtime.

I hid in the hallway to watch as my Brother, Father and both Uncles sat themselves on the kitchen floor. Uncle Martin went first, pulling his pants down in the dark kitchen. Opa stood at the ready with a large match. I heard the familiar sound of a fart, and the kitchen glowed a soft blue. Martin yelled out in Dutch. " Jezus Christus verbrand je de haren uit mijn kont." (More or less means you're burning the hair off my ass) Everyone in the house roared.

My Brother and my Dad both kept their pants on when they set fire to their farts. Surprisingly, no one was hurt or caught fire. At the end of the evening, the superior gas producing powers of my Mom's brussel sprouts were praised by all.

Black Friday

When I was working, I'd always try to get Black Friday off so I could take my Mom shopping. Black Friday was a huge thing to her, us. The news paper would be so full of sales brochures that it was at least twice its regular size. The stores started opening up earlier and earlier, so people would come in and shop for door busters.

I remember one year Pick and Save was open all night. Mom and I usually started at South Coast Plaza, where Sears and May Company were both opening around six am. When she could still walk, we'd spend hours going through items. When she was in a wheel chair, I'd spend the day pushing her from one sales counter to another.

I remember going to Lane Bryant and looking at all the clearance Jewelry. Mom and I both fell in love with the same necklace. No questions asked, I picked up the necklace and bought it for Mom. She lit up like a Christmas tree. "Oh, it's so beautiful, let me wear it, let me wear it." The sale's clerk smiled at my Mom's enthusiasm and handed her the necklace.

Mom loved Jewelry. All day long, she'd stop every once in a while to look at her new necklace. When she did, She'd hug it and blow me a kiss. Then she'd return to the serious business of shopping.

After my Mom died, I was never able to return to South Coast Plaza on Black Friday. While I tried once to go Black Friday Shopping with my husband Johnnie, it was next to impossible to get him out of bed before 10am. When I tried going by myself, the crowds only made me miss my Mother more. There was no one to watch haggling over prices, no one to watch oohing and aahing at all the beautiful things, it wasn't the same without her.

I remember days when Mom would take out her jewelry boxes and place them all on her bed. I'd lay next to her on Dad's bed and listen as she described in great detail where each and every piece was from, and why it was special to her.

I didn't know it at the time, but the vast majority of Mom's pieces were junk, costume jewelry. She had some good pieces, but those were few and far between. The stories she told were special. Her love for the jewelry was special. Seeing Mom happy was wonderful.

Five Days a Week

Mom lived to shop. After Dad died, and I quit my job, I'd take Mom shopping on most weekdays. During the Dog days of Summer, when the heat was more than either of us could bear, we'd go off to South Coast Plaza for the Day.

We'd stay in the house until around 1pm, when it started getting hot inside house. Too hot to stay at home. I'd put Mom in her wheel chair and push her to the bus stop. We'd wait outside in the sweltering heat, hoping the bus came quickly. When we got to South Coast Plaza I loved the moment we opened the big doors and were hit with a blast of cold air.

It was cool and clean and pleasant inside. I happily pushed my Mom from one end of the mall to the other. When she wanted me to stop, she'd grab hold of her wheel and point at this or that. We'd laugh and talk and walk for hours.

When I got tired of pushing, we'd take a break at Carl's Jr., where we'd order a soda and sit down. If we had some extra cash, we'd share a plate from the all you could eat salad bar. The manager never complained, or turned us away. We were there five days a week, knew everyone there, and they knew our sad financial situation.

Five days a week we sat at Carl's. Mom loved watching people walking in and out of South Coast Plaza. Carl's was located in the middle of everything. Mom would comment on this person or that, talk about the weather, and reminisce. Some days Mom brought the paper to read. Other days she'd sit and write letters. She knew the names of almost everyone who worked there. At Christmas she brought gifts of chocolate for everyone.

Once when we went to Carl's and were too broke to even buy a soda, the Manager brought us a tray with two soda cups and some burgers and fries. "We had some extra", he said while handing me the tray. When the manager left, I hugged my Mom. We were both crying at the time.

Snapshots from a Broken Camera

Mom's Love Affair with Thrift Stores and Shopping

More than anything else, Mom loved prowling thrift stores. She could happily spend hours digging for hidden treasure. When I was about three years old, Mom found a full length mink stole at the Disabled American Veterans thrift store. At least that's what she said it was. She adored that thing.

When I was a kid, Mom bought a good portion of my clothing from thrift stores. I've always had unusually long legs, so the pants my Mom purchased for me were rarely long enough. So I was heckled and laughed at by mean spirited kids at school.

When I complained my pants were too low, Mom said I was wearing them too high. So I got in the habit of wearing the pants down low around my hips, the crotch a good 3 to 6 inches below its normal place. This way the pant leg bottoms made it down at least to my ankles. The problem was, I'd generally end up tearing the crotch. At which point my Mom told me I wasn't walking like a lady, and it was my fault all my pants were tearing.

Kmart's High Water Pants

When Kmart opened up next to our house, my pant situation didn't get much better. You see Mom always bought sale items. For reasons I will never know, there were always a lot of half size pants in Kmart's clearance racks. So Mom decided they were good enough for me. Half size clothing are made specifically for short people. While I'm not exactly tall, my legs always have been long. So my Kmart pants looked like culottes, and were way too short to pull down. A lot of kids teased me about my "high water" pants.

If I complained Mom told me my clothes were good enough for me, and certainly good enough for school. You are growing too fast Jeanne, girl's clothing is expensive, so these will do. Why then do I remember Mom getting new clothing for my brother at Sears Roebuck and J.C. Penny and Montgomery Ward?

I was in my late teens before I discovered tall sizes. Oh my God, pants that fit, what a revelation! Not surprisingly Mom, used to seeing me in short pants, said these looked too long. But I didn't care. I was glad to be wearing pants which actually fit.

Mom would scour the newspaper for sales and coupons and deals. She loved Hummel figurines. I remember Sears had a sale of imitation Hummels. Good enough for Mom she happily purchased one of each.

Good enough was a term I learned to despise. Cheap silver plated bread boxes that sort'a kind'a looked expensive, good enough as gifts for Mom's friends. Cheap imitation crystal vases and bowls that almost looked real, good enough as gifts for Mom's friends.

Our house was filled all sorts of Cheap imitation things, way too many things, cheap knick knacks, and cheap paper reprints of paintings set in cheap plastic frames. Mom mixed everything together, displayed beautiful real things with atrociously bad junk. She believed if she displayed everything together, that people would believe it was ALL real.

Cheap was good, cheap made Mom happy, cheap allowed Mom to buy lots of good enough things. So she purchased cheap sheets so rough they made my skin hurt, cheap cuts of meat that had to be cooked or boiled for hours, cheap shampoo, cheap tooth brushes. Cheap tooth brushes that were supposed to last, but rarely did.

Thinking back, the times I remember Mom happiest, was when I was taking care of her. Which in a way is kind of sad for both of us. She'd get angry if I skipped one of our "Mom's day out" so I could go out on a date. Not that I dated much.

Once when I was going on a date, Mom pitched such a fit that I actually agreed to take her with me. I apologized when I picked him up at his house. (He didn't have a car at the time).

Mom planted herself in the front seat and refused to talk to my date. When we got to the movie theatre, Mom sat between the two of us. When I tried talking to my date, she'd scoot forward in her seat making it impossible for the two of us to talk. After the movie was over I dropped off Mom at Denny's, where she and my Dad ate dinner most week nights. She exited my car glowering at me.

Mom was Mom. While I hated the things she did to me, I still loved her. Life with Mom was complicated, by any standard.

☙Win Lose

When I was studying to become a respiratory therapist, the school that I attended had a weight requirement. Before I could graduate I had to lose at least 50 pounds. I attended that school for almost two years. It took me a little over a year to lose 120 pounds.

For an all too brief instant I was actually normal looking. I weighed 140 pounds and had a 22 inch waist. I wore regular clothing and looked good. Men asked me on dates. I could jog, play sports and suddenly found myself surrounded with friends.

After reaching my target weight, I took ALL my old FAT clothing and tossed it in the trash. I couldn't believe I could walk into ANY store I wanted to buy clothing. Clothing that actually fit! I went on a new clothing orgy!

I maintained that weight for about five years. Then I came down with a bladder infection and herpes. I didn't know it at the time, but the doctor who treated me was a slime bag and an idiot.

He started me on massive steroid injections (to cure my herpes) and performed weekly gynecological treatments which consisted of popping each and every herpes sore. He then painted each sore with Methylene Blue dye (used for microscope slides).

He told me he was the only doctor in the world who could cure herpes.

Over the course of six months I gained almost 100 pounds. I looked freakish and swollen. Then suddenly without comment my doctor closed up shop and stopped my treatments. After months of weekly steroid injections he stopped me cold turkey.

A week or so I returned to my apartment from work and found myself unable to walk. I had a fever of 106. I went to the E.R. and they ran all sorts of tests. My bladder infection had returned and had spread to my kidneys. The herpes had spread to the inside of my vagina. I was a mess.

It took me YEARS to recover my physical health. I continued working, but suffered constant infections. I almost lost a kidney. I was on and off antibiotics for years. The doctor who treated me lost his license. It wasn't until decades later I learned his treatments were responsible for my weight gain and the loss of my health.

For about a year I became too ill to work as a respiratory therapist. I went on state disability and was forced to move back home.

I remember telling my Mom I needed to buy clothing which fit better. My Mom, happy as a lark told me to follow her. She took me to her bedroom closet and took down out a huge pile of clothing.

"For you my darling." She gushed excitedly. She handed me an armful of clothing, still on hangers. *"I saved these for you."*

I looked at the clothing and began to cry. My Mom was grinning like some sort of insane Cheshire cat. Six years prior, my Mom had taken it upon herself to rescue every piece of FAT clothing I'd thrown away. She'd kept them hidden in her closet all these years.

"Why in God's name did you pull all my clothing out of the trash?"

"For you my darling! I did it for you. I knew you'd never be able to stay skinny. You were fat before. I knew it was only a matter of time before you were fat again. So I saved ALL these just for you. Aren't you happy I saved them?"

I grabbed one of my old tops and held it out to my Mom. *"Are you interested in this?"*

Snapshots from a Broken Camera

"No, that's not my style."

"You sure you don't want it Mom?" Mom shook her head no.

"OK, now don't get upset."

I went to my room and grabbed a pair of scissors, then I cut the top in half.

"Jeannika, stop that now!"

"I asked you if you wanted it and you said no. This was, is, MY top and I'm throwing it away."

"Then I will keep your clothing."

"Why keep a bunch of clothing you'll never wear Mom?"

"I'll keep them for you, for when you're too poor to buy new clothing. These will be good enough for you then!"

That afternoon I cut up all my old clothing and then threw it away AGAIN. My Mom never let me forget how stupid she thought I was for having done so.

✒ Conversations with my Selves

Living with M.P.D. [Multiple Personality Disorder], D.I.D. [Dissociative Identity Disorder] and/or P.T.S.D. [Post Traumatic Stress Disorder] sucks.

Memories, my memories, memories of abuse, pain, illness and worse define me. Me. I am a whore child, stupid, useless, dirt, shit, ugly, worthless, Mama's little bitch, cursed, hated, untouchable, unlovable, lost and eternally alone.

Abuse physical. Abuse sexual. Abuse psychological. Abuse neglect. One of everything there is ... I take the prize. Because of what was done to me and what I have done to myself. I believe ... no one can ... no one will ... no one has ... ever truly loved me.

Over the years various people (family included) have told me:

> I chose this life, my parents, and my abuse, long before I was born.
> I am paying for past sins, sins which reside within me to this day.
> Sins which prove God hates me.
> Sins which explain why God has cursed me.
> I allowed the abuse to go on.
> I caused the abuse.
> I seduced my abusers.
> I deserved my abuse.
> I could have fought harder.
> I could have spoken up.
> I could have walked away.
> My memories aren't real.
> I imagined and made up EVERYTHING.

Everyday I live in pain. Pain physical. Pain emotional. Pain unending and impossible to explain to *normal* people. ***Normal people expect me to live life as they do***. People who grew up safe and loved and protected. Normal people who tell me the past is in the past. Normal people who tell me the abuse is over. Normal people who expect me to forget and get on with my life, so I pretend.

Snapshots from a Broken Camera

Memories Live On Inside Me

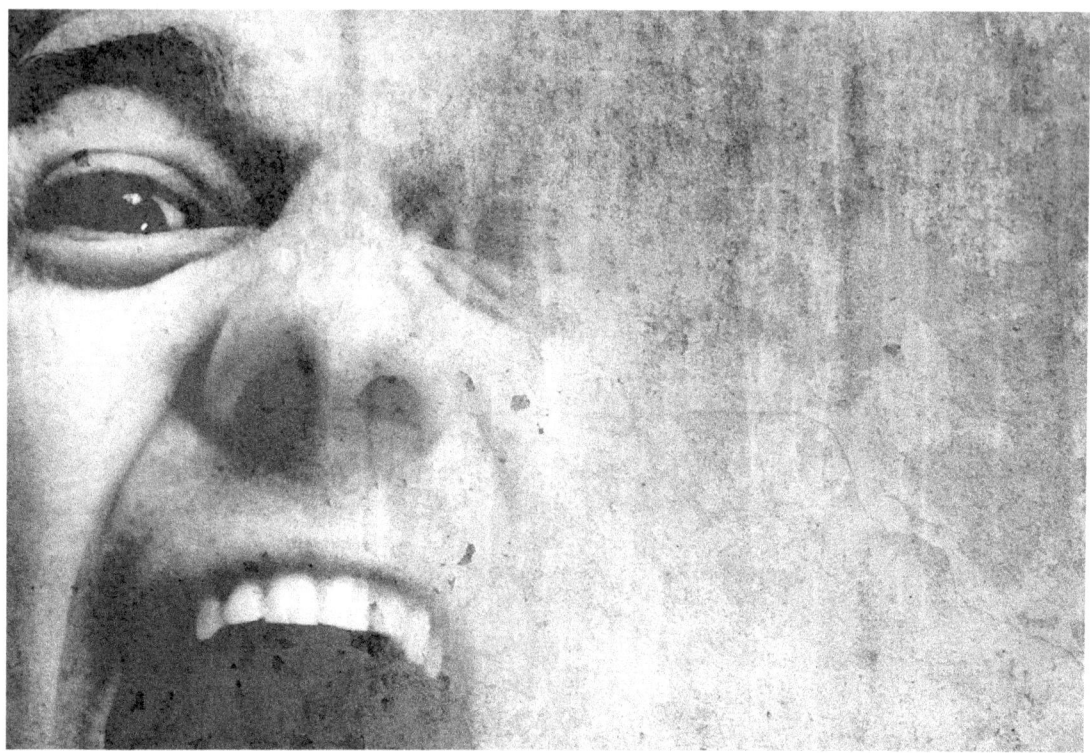

How can I explain what flashback feel like for me? How can I explain that I can't control when memories return, how they manifest, let alone the strong feelings which come with them?

I close my eyes and I'm there ... 1957, 1958, 1959, 1960 ... pick a year ... ANY year ... and I can go there. The shattering part is being there, smelling the air around me, feeling the heat or feeling the cold, seeing dead pets, hearing long dead family members talking, standing next to them, almost but not quite able to touch and hold them. I'm there, vividly, intensely, achingly there. Then just as suddenly, I take a breath, blink an eye, and I'm here and everyone is still dead.

Some days when the flashbacks are particularly intense, and I'm home alone, the little one inside me roams the house calling out for lost family members. Some days the terror she feels is so intense it feels as if my soul will shatter into a million pieces.

Some days all it takes is a tune on the radio, a particular shade of sky, the taste of vanilla ice cream, a word, a gesture or a time of day. My mind enters a time warp, my vision fades from now to back then, and for all intensive purposes I have exited into the past.

How I ironic, that the only family member I have left is totally beyond my reach. I have no words to express how much I miss my brother. My family lives on in flashbacks and dreams. In flashbacks my family is with me and I am not alone. It's not the flashbacks that hurt, it's returning to NOW which makes me wish I were dead.

Jeanne

Some days it feels as if nobody knows I'm here. I don't know how to put it into words. Some days I feel so alone I can hardly breathe.

I miss my family. I miss my Mom. I miss my Dad. I miss my Brother. I miss my grandparents.

I don't know what I did wrong. Why everyone's gone or why my Brother doesn't love me anymore.

I don't know what I did wrong. I guess must be a really bad person, who does bad things. I wish I could understand what I did so I could make it better. Things I mean, make things better.

Mama used to tell me how awful I was. Sometimes she told me I was special. Too often she would tell me I was a stupid thoughtless selfish little girl who never thought about anyone but herself. I tried, really I did, but I don't think I ever got it right. She said people would hate me and she was right. I hate me to. People like me should be punished. People like me should be killed dead.

I'm selfish. I think about myself too much. I hate feeling like no one loves me. I hate feeling stupid and dirty and ugly and bad and worthless. I'd do better if I just knew what I had to do. But it doesn't matter, because I'll never get it right and people will always hate me.

Mama used to slam the door in my face. Mama used to tell me she didn't love me. Mama used to tell me no one will ever love a girl like me. I used to pray it wasn't true, that people could love me, would love me. But I don't know.

Snapshots from a Broken Camera

Fatty fatty pants on fire

Mama used to tell me I was fat and ugly. Mama told the doctor I was fat because I ate too much candy and junk. After visiting the doctor Mama always took me for a treat. Mama took me to Seely's Bakery for cookies, or got me a big hot fudge sundae at the restaurant by the house.

"What about the doctor Mama?" I'd ask.

"This is for JUST today darling." purred Mama lovingly "You can start your diet tomorrow."

But tomorrow never came. Mama piled my plates with as much food as my Dad and older Brother. Fridays were for all you could eat fish at Thrifty's. Special weekends were for the smorgasbord. "Eat more" said Mama, "so we get our money's worth". Mama got mad at me when I couldn't finish it all. Shopping meant eating at Newberry's, grilled cheese sandwiches with oily fries, root-beer floats and Butterfinger bars.

When I got fatter, my doctor would berate my Mom for allowing me to eat so much. "It's not my fault doctor, I swear to you. It's not my fault she loves cookies and cakes and ice cream so much. She eats all the time. She eats so much I can't stop her."

"Fat is healthy doctor, healthier than how thin she used to be." Insisted my Mom.

"No it's not Mother, your daughter isn't healthier. She's still anemic and she still has rickets." Answered the doctor.

"If she looks healthy, she is healthy." And so ended the conversation. I still had chronic diarrhea, still vomited after eating out, and still felt sick.

I don't understand

I miss my Brother. I wish I knew why he doesn't want anything to do with me. After my Brother got married, Mama said she was scared to ask him things. She told me she was afraid he'd stop talking to her, like he had in the past. She didn't want to die without him.

When Johnnie's brother Tom poisoned my food no one in the family believed me. When I got sick, Tom told me and anyone else who would listen that I was crazy. When Tom tried to kill me, I had nowhere to go.

When I was sick and didn't have any place to go I called my brother to ask if I could stay. He said no. He said his house was too small. He said he didn't have an extra room.

He said that there was only room for him and his wife Angie and their dogs. I said all I needed was a sofa. He still said no. He said he knew a friend who could help me. He said he'd call a friend and get back to me. Then he stopped taking my calls. Then he changed his phone number and never called back.

I would have given my life for my brother. I shared everything I could with him. I introduced him to my friends, let him borrow my car for a year, bought him clothing, helped him get jobs, and didn't bug him when Mom was almost too much to care for.

I don't understand why the first last and ONLY time I asked for help, my brother dumped me. I got sicker and sicker and sicker.

Cameron saved me

Cameron found me, us out cold on my office floor and took us to his welding shop. He made me breathe again by breathing in my mouth when my lungs stopped working. CO2 poisoning, from a gas leak in Mel's house. I slept in Cameron's shop for almost a year.

He took care of us. He saw me and knew I was there. He played music with me and told me I could be his little girl. He would hold on to me and sing to me when I was too scared to sleep. He cried with me when I was sad. The best part was that he loved me and I felt safe and warm. I hadn't felt safe and warm for a long long time.

Cameron took me to special doctors and fed me special food to make me feel better. He took me to his family and showed me his friends. We played music and went places and joined an orchestra. I was getting healthy.

People say and do things and then they go away.

One day Cameron went away to. He was my special friend, who did a lot of wonderful things for me and helped me stay alive. I knew he had to go, just like I knew I had to stay here with Mel. It's just sad to lose a good friend to life struggles.

I know Cameron hasn't had an easy life. I know Cameron struggles with his own demons. I know he suffers with chronic pain, and works too hard. I hope and pray that he and his wife and family are doing well. He is a good person, who made a huge difference in my life.

Snapshots from a Broken Camera

Papa Mel

When I was staying with Cameron, I'd call Mel every day. He was my second Dad. Yeah, I know he was really Johnnie's Dad, but he was my Dad to. He had a bad heart, and stomach problems. But I got really sick in the house, so I couldn't go home.

I remember calling Johnnie every day to find out when I could come back home. Johnnie always said he was making the house clean and safe for us. Johnnie would call me when he was out to dinner with friends. Johnnie would call me on holidays to tell me how much fun he was having. He told me the house was almost clean.

When Mel got sick Jeanne said we had to go home to check on him. Cameron drove us there. We couldn't stay because the house was so dirty. The only good thing was that no one could say the mess was my fault, because I'd been gone for almost nine months. The bad thing was that Johnnie had been lying and had not been cleaning the house.

Mel was so skinny it looked like he was going to die. So Jeanne cleaned and cleaned and cleaned. She vacuumed the carpet and the hallway and the kitchen and the living room.

Mel's pink sheets were covered with so much cat hair they looked grey, it was horrid. His sheets hadn't been changed in over 9 months! Jeanne and me got so sick we had to wear a mask to breathe. Oh and we got these really big blisters all over and felt dizzy and sick. But we changed the bedding anyway. We also cleaned Mel's bathroom.

The only thing clean in Mel's bathroom was his toilet (which he cleaned). The floor was covered with hair, dust and dirt. The towels were also awful looking. There was a pile of dirty towels in the Garage (next to the washing machine). It took the whole day to wash them all.

Jeanne cooked and cooked and cooked. She cooked all the roasts in the freezer. She cooked all the pork chops in the freezer. She cooked bags and bags of other stuff. She put it all into these special plastic microwave freezer things we picked up at Target.

We made 45 special microwave dinners for Mel and filled up two whole freezer shelves in the upright freezer in the garage. Each freezer plate had different kinds of meat, potatoes or rice or pasta, and veggies. We made enough microwave plates to feed Mel for a month. The only problem was Johnnie ate the food with Mel and I had to come back and cook more.

The next month we came back and vacuumed Mel's room and changed his bedding which hadn't been changed since the last time. This time we went to Costco first and bought lots of food to cook. Jeanne cooked enough food to fill the upright freezer. 60 microwave dinners and 60 microwave lunches, enough to hold Mel for two months. This time we were so sick afterward we couldn't get out of bed for a week. We had welts the size of silver dollars all over our body.

Rather than cook for himself, Johnnie kept eating the food we cooked for Mel. Which is why all the food went so quickly and we had to come back in a month not two. Mel saw how sick we got and said we had to wear masks and gloves and other stuff so we wouldn't get so sick when we came over.

The next time we visited Mel we wore a special jump suit, gloves and a mask to breathe better. Mel's bedding was dark from pet hair again, and his room filled with dust. It took over an hour to get all the dust, pet hair and crud from his carpet. This time we showered afterward, and left the special suit at Mel's for next time. We were only sick a couple of days.

From then on we returned to cook and clean for Mel once a month. My doctors told me to stay away, because my health always took a nose dive afterward. In the end I moved back in with Mel and Johnnie, because Mel was sick and needed me to be there. So my friend Cameron told me I was stupid, made new friends and said goodbye.

But before Cameron said goodbye forever, he fixed me a special "clean room", and tore down all the weeds in the backyard and fixed a bunch of other stuff so I wouldn't get too sick at Mel's house. He would call a lot and send me his music. I miss him a lot, Cameron was a great big brother second Dad. I'm sorry Cameron felt like we abandoned him. I hope he understands how much I loved Mel and that I had to be there for him.

Snapshots from a Broken Camera

People say and do things ... and then they go away. I stayed with Mel until the end. I'm glad I did. I loved him more than I loved anyone else, even my own Dad. He was so special it hurts even thinking about him being gone.

I did everything I could to take care of him and keep him healthy. I'm sorry I couldn't do more. When he died the biggest and best part of me died with him. I'm with Johnnie now, who doesn't know I'm here. Nobody knows I'm here, or cares if I live or die. I miss both my Dads, I miss Cameron and I miss my Greyhound Junior.

Jeannika

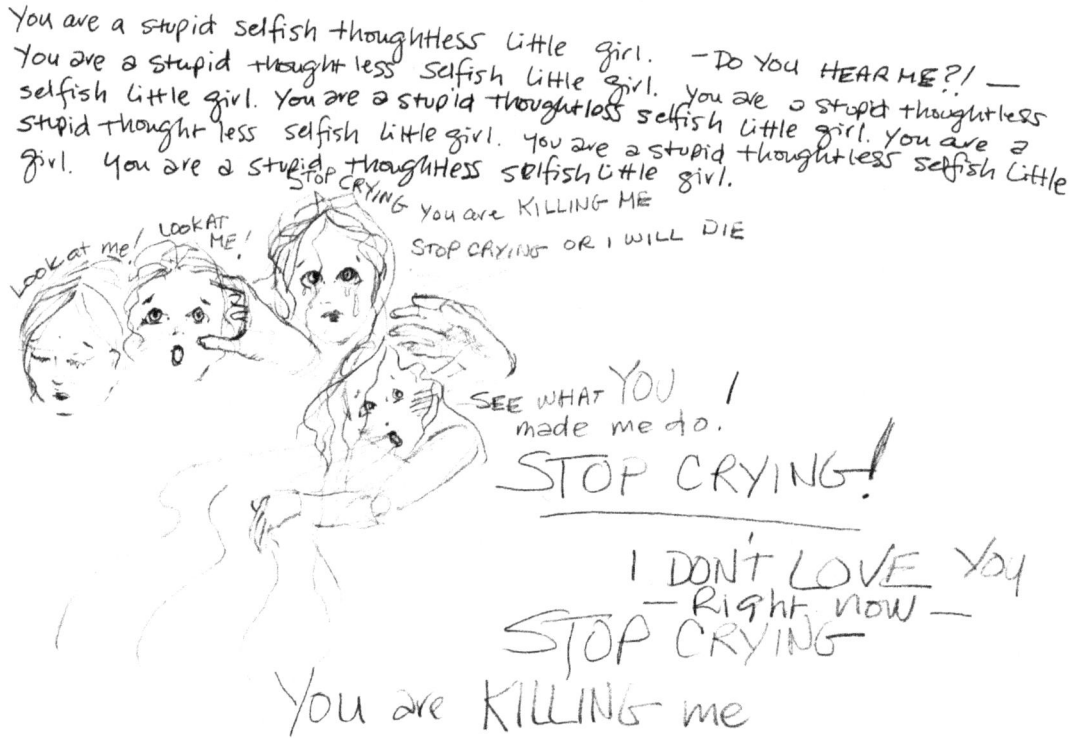

Are You Listening?

You are a stupid thoughtless selfish little bitch ... a stupid thoughtless selfish little bitch ... a stupid thoughtless selfish little bitch ... a stupid thoughtless selfish little bitch ... a stupid thoughtless selfish little bitch ... a stupid thoughtless selfish little bitch ... a stupid thoughtless selfish little bitch ... a stupid thoughtless selfish little bitch ...

Look at me!

You are a stupid thoughtless selfish little bitch ... a stupid thoughtless selfish little bitch ... a stupid thoughtless selfish little bitch ... a stupid thoughtless selfish little bitch ... a stupid thoughtless selfish little bitch ... a stupid thoughtless selfish little bitch ... a stupid thoughtless selfish little bitch ... a stupid thoughtless selfish little bitch ...

STOP CRYING!

You are a stupid thoughtless selfish little bitch ... a stupid thoughtless selfish little bitch ... a stupid thoughtless selfish little bitch ... a stupid thoughtless selfish little bitch ... a stupid thoughtless selfish little bitch ... a stupid thoughtless selfish little bitch ... a stupid thoughtless selfish little bitch ... a stupid thoughtless selfish little bitch ...

[slapping child HARD on the face]

SEE WHAT YOU MADE ME DO?!

Do You Want More?

You are a stupid thoughtless selfish little bitch ... a stupid thoughtless selfish little bitch ... a stupid thoughtless selfish little bitch ... a stupid thoughtless selfish little bitch ... a stupid thoughtless selfish little bitch ... a stupid thoughtless selfish little bitch ... a stupid thoughtless selfish little bitch ... a stupid thoughtless selfish little bitch ...

Stop crying or I'll REALLY give you something to cry about!

You are a stupid thoughtless selfish little bitch ... a stupid thoughtless selfish little bitch ... a stupid thoughtless selfish little bitch ... a stupid thoughtless selfish little bitch ... a stupid thoughtless selfish little bitch ... a stupid thoughtless selfish little bitch ... a stupid thoughtless selfish little bitch ... a stupid thoughtless selfish little bitch ...

SHUT UP ... SHUT UP ... SHUT UP - You are Killing ME - SHUT UP

If you DON'T SHUT UP - I'll send you away, you'll never see me or Daddy or your brother again.

STOP CRYING OR I WILL DIE

You are a stupid thoughtless selfish little bitch ... a stupid thoughtless selfish little bitch ... a stupid thoughtless selfish little bitch ... a stupid thoughtless selfish little bitch ... a stupid thoughtless selfish little bitch ... a stupid thoughtless selfish little bitch ... a stupid thoughtless selfish little bitch ... a stupid thoughtless selfish little bitch ...

Snapshots from a Broken Camera

I don't love you right now!

I don't love you ... You are killing me ... I don't love you ... Stop crying or I'll die ... I don't love you ... Stop crying or I'll leave ... I don't love you ... You'll NEVER SEE ME AGAIN ... I don't love you ... You are killing me killing me killing me killing me ... I don't love you ... I don't love you ... I don't love you ... I don't love you ... I don't love you ... I don't love you ...

[Mama put on her lipstick, lit a cigarette, then grabbed her purse and gloves.]

I'm leaving, you are killing me with all your tears and drama, you don't give a damn about anyone but yourself. I don't love you right now ...

I don't love you ... You are killing me ... I don't love you ... Stop crying or I'll die ... I don't love you ... Stop crying or I'll leave ... I don't love you ... You'll NEVER SEE ME AGAIN ... I don't love you ... You are killing me killing me killing me killing me ... I don't love you ... I don't love you ... I don't love you ... I don't love you ... I don't love you ... I don't love you ...

Please don't leave me ~ Please don't go!

"Mama, please don't leave. I'm sorry Mama, I'll do anything you say. I love you. Please don't leave."

Pushing her daughter aside, Mama walked briskly toward the front door, her cigarette leaving a long slender trail of smoke.]

" Mama, please don't leave, I love you, I'm sorry, please love me. "

[Mama's five inch stiletto heels clicked loudly on the hardwood floor. The front door creaked open, then slammed quickly shut]

" Mama, please don't leave, I love you, I'm sorry, please love me. "

[Outside the car door creaked opened and shut ... a minute later the engine purred to life. A second later the car began jerking forward.]

I stood hugging the front door, my face pressed against the hard cold glass. I wept loudly as I watched Mama's car pull out of the driveway. When I could no longer see her car, I slid down the front door onto the hardwood floor. No longer human, no longer part of the world ... I pressed my face and hands against the bottom of the door.

Time stopped as I sat, locked in a pointless embrace, for all eternity. My bruised and tattered soul melted slowly into the door's wooden surface. A part of me will always be there, wooden, cold, shattered and alone, waiting for Mama to return.

"Don't leave Mama. I'm sorry, I love you I'll be good, please don't hate me." I whispered one last time to the door and the floor, and then vanished into the wood. Two hours later when my Mother returned, there was nothing to be seen but wood.

Throughout 10 unbearable years of ugly words and threats followed by dramatic exits, no one ever felt my pain, heard my sobs, or saw my tears. I can still hear Mama telling me she didn't love me and calling me a stupid thoughtless selfish little girl.

Snapshots from a Broken Camera

GiGi

Mama was angry with me a lot.

- Mama angry meant hard slaps on the face that left me seeing stars.
- Mama angry meant telling me I was bad or stupid or ugly or selfish.
- Mama angry meant shaking me so hard my head hurt.
- Mama angry meant everything was always my fault.
- Mama angry meant locking me in my room.
- Mama angry meant forcing me to eat food that made me sick, and then telling me I was a bad girl for getting sick.

Mama told me I was bad so many times I believed I was beyond repair. It was confusing though, some days I was her precious "Golden Girl", whom she loved with all her heart. Other days she told me I was stupid, ugly, selfish, thoughtless and totally worthless.

Mama angry meant Pussy Willow had to die.

When my Grandfather Opa was in the hospital I begged Mama to save my cat Pussy Willow. Mama told me Pussy Willow was just a cat. Mama told me she wouldn't spend cash money to save a God damned cat. Not when Her Dad was dying.

Mama said cats were plentiful and easy to replace, Opa was not. Cats weren't worth spending a lot of money on. Mama told me her Father was dying and I was a stupid thoughtless selfish little bitch for bothering her. Daddy didn't say anything.

Pussy Willow couldn't pee and his whole body got big and hard and swollen. It took him a long time to die. He hurt so bad I couldn't hold him or touch him. He died in a box in the backyard, howling in pain. He wasn't even a year old. I still have nightmares about him dying.

Mama angry meant not drinking too much water.

When I was little I used to be thirsty a lot. I was so little that I couldn't reach the sink, or open the fridge to get water. I couldn't reach the faucet handles in bathroom sink. So I'd climb up the kitchen laundry hamper, stand up on the sink and grab a new cup, fill it with water and drink. Mama wanted me to use the same cup to drink water all day long. She got mad when I used a cup for each drink. She said I was making too many dishes for her. She also said drinking too much water makes me pee too much and use too much toilet paper.

To this day I have to force myself to drink water.

Mama angry meant not taking long baths.

I love taking baths. I love hot soapy water. I love the way sound echoes in the bathroom.

When I was little my Mom made my Brother and I take baths together. My Brother had cool toys and told stories. I loved being in the tub with him so much I didn't want to get out.

One winter night Mama told us it was time to get out. I complained and asked if I could PLEASE stay a little longer.

"NO"

"Please Mama"

"NO, get out now."

Snapshots from a Broken Camera

I kept playing and pretended not to hear. Suddenly the bathroom was filled with loud noise. Cold hard water was falling down on me from the ceiling. My Brother vaulted out of the bathtub. At the same time Mama pulled out the plug and slammed shut the glass doors in front of the tub.

I had never been in a shower before and was terrified beyond words. The water was so cold it made me shiver all over and made my heart beat in a funny way. I screamed and screamed and screamed. Mama was laughing really loud. She sounded like she was having troubling breathing. She'd laugh and take in a noisy breath of air. The sound scared me.

I tried getting out of the bathtub, but the glass door wouldn't slide open. I tried to get away from the cold hard water. I ran back and forth in the tub, screaming and banging on the glass door. "Let me out LET ME OUT" I screamed in terror. Mama kept laughing.

By the time Mama let me out of the tub I was covered with bruises (from falling against the water spout), and my fingers and toes were blue from the ice cold water. "That will teach you to get out of the tub when I tell you to." Mama was still laughing when I ran into my room naked and shivering. My brother had gone to bed.

I was almost 17 before I was able to take regular showers without having panic attacks. To this day I'm scared to take a shower in a hotel. A year later when Mama and Papa took us to see the movie Psycho I got even more scared of showers.

Mama angry meant learning to hate my body.

I grew up in Santa Ana. A number of times a year we'd get "Santa Ana" winds. Lovely warm wind that tossed leaves, made trees dance and felt wonderful (to me at least).

I experienced my first Santa Ana wind when I was three. It was so amazing I thought it could lift me into the sky. The wind was so strong it filled up my blouse and lifted it part way up. Each time the wind tugged up my blouse it made me smile, so I took my blouse off and the wind blew it up into our backyard.

The wind felt like a thousand soft warm hugs against my skin. So I took off all my clothing and began running up and down the street waiting for the wind to pick me up and blow me into our backyard.

I didn't know that a neighbor called up Mama and told her I was running around naked. Mama came outside screaming for me to come inside. Mama grabbed me and slapped my bottom, then dragged me into the house.

Mama shoved me in my room. The floor was cold, my room was cold so I went to get dressed.

"NO" screamed Mama "You wanted to run around naked like a whore ... so stay naked"

"But Mama I'm cold."

"You should have thought about that BEFORE you took off all your clothing."

I pulled back the covers on my bed and began crawling inside.

"NO" came Mama's reply. "I'm going to teach you a lesson. You will lay ON TOP of your bed, NAKED like a whore, until I tell you to get dressed."

"But Mama, I'm cold."

Mama slapped me on the face. *"Filthy Whore!"*

I lay on top of my bed for what felt like an eternity. I shivered and cried and begged Mama to let me get dressed. I felt more alone and ashamed than I'd ever felt before.

From that day on, even the thought of being naked filled me with terror. The shame, terror and panic I felt was so bad, I couldn't take communal showers in high school or college. To this day I'm unable to sleep or walk around unclothed.

A Day at the Beach

The first time I went to the beach I fell in love with seagulls and the smell of the ocean. I watched with wonder as these beautiful white creatures hovered over me. With my stubby toddler arms outstretched ... I ran and ran and ran and ran ... hoping the wind would pick me up and carry me up to play with the gulls.

The sand was funny and made me fall. I'd run and fall and run and fall and run some more. When we went home, my body, hair and clothing were all covered with sand.

Mama said there was too much sand on me for the bathtub. When we got home Mama put me into the utility sink next to the washing machine. She scrubbed and scrubbed and scrubbed and scrubbed. Mama told me she thought I would never get clean.

Snapshots from a Broken Camera

The Douche Bag

My Mom started douching me when I was three years old. She filled her big red douche bag with cold tap water and hung it on a nail at the top of the left kitchen cabinet. Then she opened her ironing board and placed the pointed end over the kitchen sink.

She picked me up and lay me down naked, face up, with my bare feet hanging down into the sink. She used one white wand to clean the inside of my lady parts. She pushed another white wand up inside my butt.

I experienced my first episode of bacterial vaginosis, with vaginal drainage a week or so later. The skin alongside my legs and vaginal area became red and inflamed. It was a horrible and painful time. I received no treatment for this infection, other than more frequent douching.

My Mom continued douching me for some time. Always when she and I were home alone. I was always afraid I was going to fall off the ironing board. The water wasn't warm, so sometimes I got cramps and cried and shivered. I was always scared. If I tried to move or get up my Mother pinned me down. Once she used a belt to strap me onto the board.

Years later, when I asked my Mom why she had douched me when I was little, she looked at me like I was crazy. She said she didn't know what I was talking about. If I pressed on, she always said, "you must have dreamed it". While I may well be crazy, I never dreamt being douched by my Mother. All the times she douched me, I never saw her soak or clean the bag and wands in anything but water.

I am sensitive to bleach and other detergents. My Dad's underwear got dirty a lot. He said he had wet farts, which always cracked me up. So Mom had to use a lot of bleach in the wash when she cleaned his underpants.

The problem is, I can't wear clothing that's been bleached. When I wear underwear that's been bleached, my skin gets red and oozy. I guess when I was little Mom must have washed my undies with bleach, because my skin was always red and sore.

When I was in my early teens my Mom let me wash my own underwear. I didn't use bleach and the contact dermatitis finally ended. I think my Mom realized then I was sensitive to bleach and stopped using it when she did my laundry. I never did learn why my Mom douched me.

Hugs and kisses

I like giving hugs. Hugs are for telling people you love them. Hugs are for telling people to feel better. Hugs are for making sad people feel warm and safe and loved. I used to crawl into Amy and Opa's lap for hugs. Opa hugged me and gave me special Dutch cookies.

When Mama was sick, or angry, or busy, or sad, she would get mad when I tried to hug her.

If I asked for too many hugs, Mama would push me away. Sometimes she would scream at me.

Mama gave all sorts of different hugs. Sometimes

Hugs I couldn't escape ... hugs that hurt and squeezed the air out of my lungs. If I tried to push away, Mama got angry and hugged me tighter, or slapped me in the face. When she was happy, Mama gave tender hugs, filled with butterfly kisses. When Mama was sad she'd hold me gently and sometimes cry. I never knew what kind of hugs to expect.

I miss Mama, and I'm sorry she died. But I'm glad she can't hurt or scare me anymore.

Story time

I like talking to people. When I was really little I talked all the time. I talked to everyone. When I was visiting, Amy said didn't like me talking to strangers. Amy told me bad people would hurt me if talked too much. She said strangers loved eating little girls for dinner. Amy told me if I talked to strangers, one might grab me and take me away from home.

When I asked My Mama what a stranger would do to me, she said he would kill me. When I asked Mama why. She told me it was because strangers love eating little girls. Mama said little girls have soft tasty meat. Mama said if a stranger got me he would cut me into little pieces with a big knife. Mama said the stranger would eat my feet and cook the rest of me in a big pan.

After that I didn't like going outside Amy and Opa's house. I was afraid of the strangers that lived in her neighborhood. When I was three we moved across town and I stopped being afraid of going outside. I was happy I could be friends with the mailman again. I was happy I could talk with everyone I saw.

Snapshots from a Broken Camera

Little Boys with Twigs

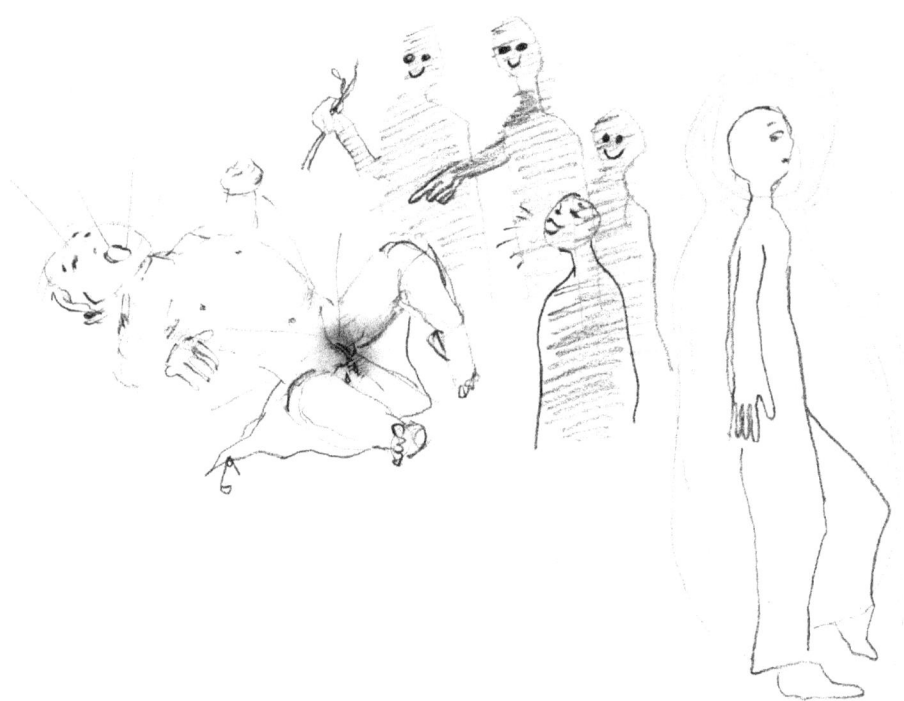

When I was a toddler, and still in diapers, Mama left me at my Grandmother's house. At that time we lived across the street, and Oma often watched me when Mama went shopping. Today was no different.

Daddy was at work, so Mama didn't access to the car. Opa worked, and he couldn't drive her either, so Mama walked to the store. Mama walked to the store a lot. Sometimes, when I was lucky, she took my brother and I with her. Me in my stroller, and my brother ambling along.

That afternoon, when my brother returned from school, Oma told us to go in the yard to play.

Oma and Opa had a magical backyard filled with fruit trees and every kind of flower imaginable. Among his many talents, Opa was an award winning horticulturalist. He had a magic citrus tree which grew oranges, tangerines and grapefruit. He made it by grafting branches from other types of citrus trees.

Opa had a hundred million hummingbird feeders around the outside of his house and backyard. In the summer Opa's backyard was filled with hummingbirds. There were red and blue and green hummingbirds. Hummingbirds hovered over vines and flowers and tree branches. Hummingbirds were drinking bright red sugar water from Opa's feeders. I loved the soft clicking noise hummingbirds made, and watching them zip from place to place.

I remember I was watching hummingbirds in Opa's backyard when a group of boys came over to play with my Brother. I don't think my Brother liked watching me. I'm sure he'd rather be out playing with his friends than watching me.

When a little boy I didn't know pulled down my diapers I wasn't afraid. I was so little, people were always taking my diapers off to change them. I'd lay back, like always, and wait for it to be done. When the little boy pointed to me and laughed, the other boys laughed with him, so I smiled and laughed with them. When the little boy pushed me onto the dirt, I couldn't see my brother and was afraid.

The little boys stood around me in a circle. I couldn't understand what they were saying or what they were laughing about. But they looked and sounded friendly, so I smiled and continued laughing with them. I couldn't see my brother.

One of the little boys started inserting small twigs inside my vaginal opening. The twigs felt rough and uncomfortable. The little boys laughs grew louder. I tried getting up, but it hurt. Some of the twigs fell out, others pinched my insides. When I started to cry the boys vanished, leaving me to toddle naked in Oma and Opa's driveway.

"Amy" (my name for Oma) I cried loudly, my brother nowhere to be found. When I saw Amy run towards me, I was flooded with relief. I ran to her, hoping she would make it stop hurting. Instead Oma smacked me on my face and bottom. She yanked the twigs out of me, and began screaming. Screaming at me in Dutch, using words I only half understood. "Vies stoute meisje!" [Filthy nasty little girl]

She lifted me from the ground and carried me into the house. My brother was on Amy and Opa's big front porch looking across the street. Oma cleaned the dirt and blood from me and put on a fresh diaper. When she was done, she looked at me with an angry face full of disgust, and pushed me into the living room.

Oma never told Mama what had happened. After that day, Amy's disgusted look became all too familiar. After that day Amy told me I was "vies" [dirty, nasty] a lot.

Snapshots from a Broken Camera

The Day The Sparkle Left my Eyes

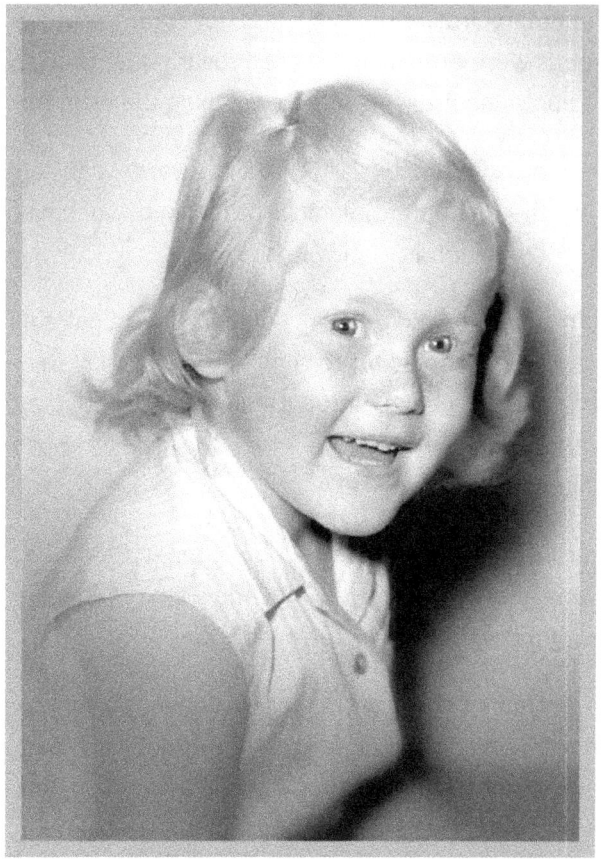

Once upon a time ... when the world was fresh and new ... my eyes would sparkle and I used to shine. I believed ~ everyday ~ was filled with miracles. Magic and fairy dust were real and I felt safe and warm and loved.

- *Before the changes,*
- *before my soul eroded to dust,*
- *before my spirit first tasted fear and death,*
- *before evil triumphed over good,*
- *before learning Santa had retired to Miami,*
- *before Mama told me Tinkerbelle wasn't real,*
- *before the changes small and large and in between*
  ~ my spirit glistened and shined.

Too Many Tears

"Too many tears", Mama had said, I had cried too many tears. I was vain and selfish and bad. Little girls need to listen their Mommies and never speak back.

But it had hurt when Mama combed my wet hair with her hard stiff bristle brush, so I always cried ... and she always told me I complained too much. When Mama pulled her hard stiff bristle brush across my head, I felt strands of hair snapping off and cried. Mama said I was being a baby and cried too much.

One day, as I sat at my piano, Mama grabbed my hair and cut it off. She cut it quickly, without warning ... before I could protest. When I complained that I looked like **"Buster Brown"**, Mama cut off more hair **"for good measure"**. The hair on my back, itched.

"I look like a boy Mama" I cried.

You look the way you deserve to look." Said Mama.

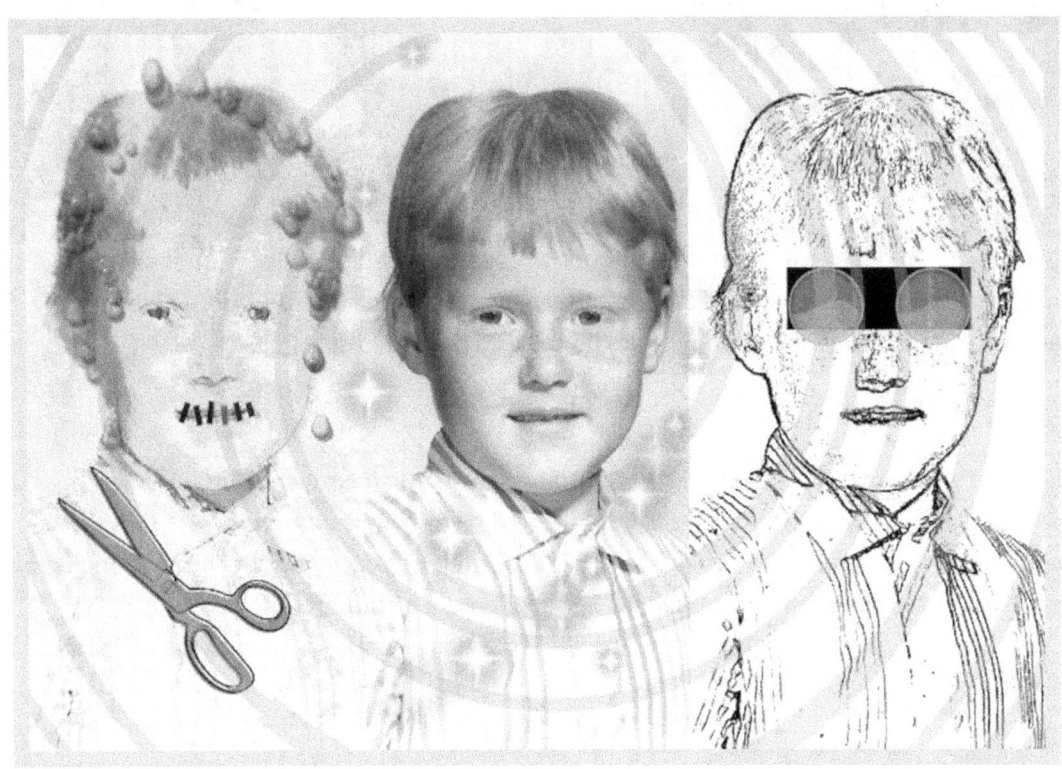

Snapshots from a Broken Camera

My ALL American Psycho Family

Growing up in the Barkemeijer de Wit family could be challenging. For a lot of different reasons. Mom was bipolar and often severely paranoid, Dad suffered from Tourettes (the act stupid and make strange sounds kind that I also have) and seizures.

Strange Child

By any 1950's American standard I was a strange child. My folks were Dutch immigrants, who spoke Dutch almost exclusively at home, as did the rest of our family. Not that they couldn't speak English, they spoke a whole lot of different languages. My brother and I grew up learning to speak Dutch, English and German, because our parents spoke Dutch, English and German. Because we grew up in Santa Ana, we also learned to speak Spanish.

Unfortunately for me I spoke English with a Dutch accent. As it turned out, other than some kids whose families had come to California from Mexico, I was the only kid in school with foreign parents. If that wasn't bad enough, I'd been born with blazing red hair, vivid green eyes, and skin the color of whole milk.

There were only two red heads in my school, and I was one of them. In a school populated largely by slender blond haired, beautifully tanned native Californian's and lovely dark skinned Hispanics, I stuck out like a very pale sore thumb.

Being four, really small, and somewhat freakish looking made me an instant target for the dreaded "big kids". The embarrassing fact that I had yet to master the rudiments of a Kindergarten toilet (with its huge alien looking u shaped black seats) by myself, made me a the subject of jokes and ridicule from the rest of my class.

I'd only JUST learned to use the potty at home. The toilet seats at school were way too big, and the toilet way too high for my tiny 4 year old butt to navigate without capsizing.

Invariably I'd end up ass down in the bottom of the toilet bowl, with my feet dangling. The only thing keeping me from a watery grave were my tiny arms wrapped around the back of the seat.

If I was lucky my teacher found me and fished me out of the toilet. On one particularly memorable day, a classmate found me, opened the door, and invited the whole class in to see the side show freak. Suffice it to say, from Kindergarten on, school was never an easy place.

Snapshots from a Broken Camera

Fear God

Mom had been a relatively well known psychic, and people often dropped by our home to get information on their lives. Mom was brutally honest to the point of being sadistic. She'd tell people things about themselves and/or their loved ones they probably would have been better not knowing. Many times I saw her words reduce people to tears.

Mom also used her psychic visions to punish me and my brother, and to keep our family in line. As the years passed, and I got a little wiser, I learned she often added her own spin to her predictions, sort'a kind'a stacking the psychic deck in her favor.

She was fond of telling me God worked for HER (not the other way around) as he was a busy guy and needed good psychics like my Mom to take care of things he didn't have time for (like our family). She swore to me that God ALWAYS told her ANYTHING I ever did that was bad. In a nut shell, I was screwed from the word go.

Forgiveness is Unattainable

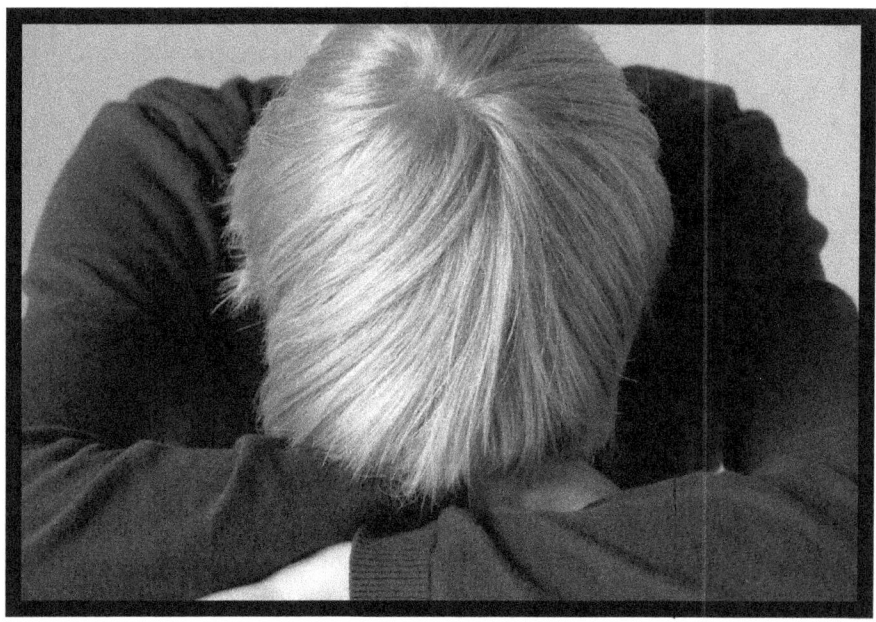

Whenever Mom thought I'd been bad, was thinking evil thoughts, or had done something I shouldn't have, she'd give me *"the look"*. Then she'd say God had told her she needed to have a special talk with me. Special talk, being her way of telling me I was in big trouble and life was about to become hell.

Most of the time I hadn't done anything at all. If I told Mom I hadn't done anything wrong she'd either say ***"good, I was just testing you."*** or slap me and accuse me of lying.

If I became scared, Mom told me that was proof I'd been bad. If I threw up with fear, she told me that was God's punishment for my having been bad. After years of fearing God's wrath, I'd actually walk up and confess to my Mom the moment I did anything wrong. I believed I was born so evil that I was born to be punished. Born to burn in Hell. Basically, God could never, would never, grant me forgiveness.

The worst part was NEVER knowing when God was going to strike. It seemed I was such a horrible Godless person that I didn't always know when I was being bad. On days when God told my Mom I'd been bad, and I didn't know what I'd done wrong and/or didn't confess, I got the full treatment. Prayers, Bible lecture, Mom lecture, and her take on what a nasty horrible child I was.

The bottom line being, I was going to hell, and Mom was the only person who could save me ... if I confessed and asked God's forgiveness.

❧ What's in a Name?

Mom told me she named me "Jeanne Sandra", after two of my grandparents.

My maternal grandmother's name was Adrianije. In the Netherlands she had been called Jeanne [pronounced Shawn in the Netherlands] by her Dutch friends, her American friends called her Jean.

So I was named Jeanne, which is really pronounced Shawn, everywhere in the world EXCEPT America, where it's pronounced Jean. Naturally my Mom kept insisting my name was pronounced "Gee knee" and told EVERYONE that's what they had to call me.

Unfortunately there's no American "J" sound in the Dutch language, so my grandparents pronounced my name Yee Nee [because that's how a Dutchman pronounced an American "J"], eventually calling me Jeannika [pronounced Yee-Nick-a]. Are you confused yet?

My paternal grandmother's name, was Sara, or Sar to her family. My Dad's mom had been born to Jewish parents, so my mother assumed Sarah was a Jewish name. (Guess she hadn't had as much bible time as she professed.) My Mom told me Sandra was the Christian American version of Sarah, which never made sense to me (or anyone else for that matter).

My Brother, who was born in the Netherlands, was named after a whole lot of people.

Our Dad's name was Heindrik (after Dad's Catholic father [Dirk] and uncle [Hein]), but then again Dad had a number of other Barkemeijer relatives named Heindrik, so who knows how accurate that story was. Also, Mom tended to embellish ANY story she told (translation: lie). So there's a good chance this story was bullshit as well.

Most of Dad's relatives either called him Heine-Mann or Hein (both way too Jewish sounding for Mom). A lot of folks started calling Dad "Dick". Mom said she named my Brother after our Dad and his grandfather Dirk. So naturally she named my brother Dick.

She decided to also name him after both her brothers "Wouter and Maarten" Which is how my Brother was named Dick Walt Martin. As he was born in the Netherlands, I don't know how my Mom came up with those variations.

My mom had an incomprehensible sense of logic, and often based important and life altering decisions on facts apparent only to her. Her choice of names, for both my brother and myself are but two tiny examples.

❧Everyone has a history

So where is mine?

I've spent the last five years trying to discover my Grandfather's history. Growing up my Mom told a story about how her Grandfather (my Great Grandfather) had been a horrible and abusive drunk. He was a carpenter who squandered every penny he made on alcohol. That his wife was forced to take in laundry to support her son (my Grandfather).

I was told She had been so poor she couldn't afford a baby sitter. So she hid my Grandfather's shoes in the winter, so he couldn't get out. That my Grandfather worked as a contractor, to pay his way through University. He earned his degree in architecture, eventually becoming wealthy after starting his own successful architectural firm.

I was told my Great Grandmother had been a simple uneducated country woman, who wore traditional Dutch clothing, cap and shoes. My Grandfather built a room for her in his home, and she lived with him until her death at age 104. Which is where my Mom's story more or less ends. The intimation was that my Grandfather had been an only child.

Today I located my maternal Grandfather's birth certificate in a box of papers I was going through. Written on it were the full names of both my Grandfather's parents.

If you have full names, there are a number of Dutch websites which will allow you to research your family history. Today I learned more than I ever expected about my Grandfather's end of the family. What I learned has left me stunned.

Snapshots from a Broken Camera

My Grandfather was the first of seven children born to Johannes Hendrik Fontijn and Neeltje Maria Wols.

One of my Grandfather's younger brother's married the sister of my Grandmother. A fact I'm amazed my Mother never brought up. A bigger question I have, is how do you hide seven siblings, wives, husbands and other assorted relatives? Why in God's earth would you want to?

But wait, it gets even better. I traced my Grandfather's lineage back a few generations and learned he's actually related to the Bode's (my Grandmother's end of the family).

It turns out I've had a pile Fontijn relatives living in the U.S. and the Netherlands I never knew about. Why were these people kept secret? Other than my Fontijn cousins, who most likely don't know either, there is no one alive I can ask.

I've always assumed the reason my Mom kept us away from my Dad's Jewish end of family, was because of their religion. Now that I've learned she also hid her own family from us, I'm wondering what she had to hide.

For me, truth is a precious commodity. When you grow up with a self absorbed and abusive Mother who's also a pathological liar, the truth becomes even more precious. I pray God I'll someday learn where I came from and who the people in my family were.

❧ Remembering Sara

My Dad's Mother Sara was born on 27 March 1889, in Amsterdam, Netherlands to Mozes and Betje Bleekrode.

Her family was Jewish. She had eight brothers and sisters, most of whom died in concentration camps (along with their families) during the war.

Other than my Grandmother, I have never met any surviving members of the Bleekrode family.

I was 57 when I learned how large my Grandmother's family had been, and how many had died in German concentration camps.

For reasons of his own, Dad rarely spoke about anyone other than his immediate family.

Picture of my Dad and my Grandparents out for a day in an Amsterdam park.

Snapshots from a Broken Camera

Who am I?

From an early age I felt as if Mom was ashamed that my brother and I were of what she called *"mixed"* blood. Mom constantly told me I was more Fontijn than Barkemeijer, that the "one quarter" (in truth half) Jewish part of me was so small as to have no bearing on who I was or ever would be.

"For God's sake Never tell people your Father is part Jew." She'd say. *"Too many people hate the Jews."* When I asked why, Mom told me that people hated Jews because they controlled so much of the world's money. She told me a lot of people wanted the Jews dead.

Mom said if I told anyone about Dad's Jewish heritage, I would be putting ALL our lives at risk. Mom believed another war was coming. She said people's hatred of Jews was so strong that when war came we could all end up dead.

I've always been an artist and a musician, always written and my Mom always told me any talent I had came from her. The fact that she couldn't play an instrument and didn't value my artistic gifts, never came into play.

The fact that there were no artists in her family, no musicians and no writers, never entered her mind. Her Father, my Grandfather, was a draftsman and an architect, which in her mind was all the proof of inheritable talent she needed.

As a child I told my Mom I wanted to be an artist and she laughed. When I was invited to join the National Children's Orchestra, she said no. It was too far away, I'd get raped or killed. When I was invited to Join the Young Americans, she said no as well. She said no when I was invited to tour Hawaii with Jack Coleman's choir. No. No. No.

When I was ready to start college, I told my Mom I wanted to major in art. As usual, her answer was a resounding NO. She argued an art major was a stupid waste of time. College (free in those days) would be wasted on me.

She said I'd just get married, have a pile of kids, at which point my life would be over. She swore I would never use what I'd learned. She made it clear she'd NEVER pay for my college education, and would NEVER pay for me to major in art. The ONLY education she'd pay for was a nursing degree, which she said would help me find a doctor husband.

"Marry a doctor" she had said. *"That way you'll never have to do it, because he'll be too tired and busy to have sex."* When I winced, she told me she was only trying to help. *"Sex leads to babies and everyone knows that once you have children, your life is over. Trust me, I should know."*

"Way to make me feel loved Mom." I thought to myself.

I eventually put myself through school (twice) respiratory therapy and computer programming. I continued to learn all I could about art, drawing, painting whenever I could. Continued with music, and taught myself to write, eventually taking college writing classes when I was in my 30s. I never valued my artistic talents, and thought I must look selfish and self absorbed to spend so much time doing things I love to do.

Irony of Ironies being the awards I garnered for my artwork, music and stories. I was 57 when I learned about my Grandmother's family. They were renown artists, musicians, writers, diamond cutters and more. One of Kleintje's brothers was a well known graphic artist, the other a world class Violinist, all were educated.

My Grandmother's friends and family were the stuff of magic, musicians the likes of Arthur Rubinstein visited her home. Yet in my Mom's eyes Dad's family members were nothing more than tiny blips on her radar.

Despite everything, I managed to learn that the Bleekrode family has been part of Amsterdam for over 600 years. Astonishingly, Bleekrode survivors of the Holocaust still reside there. Their names and stories are part of Amsterdam history.

Snapshots from a Broken Camera

Now I know what my Dad couldn't speak of, the unimaginable loss of all those he held dear. The birth of his only son, my Mom forcing him to choose between leaving his remaining family behind or never seeing his son again. Heart break upon heart break.

Mom also used the threat of leaving to convince her parents (who hadn't wanted to leave Holland) to emigrate to America. She was going to America, no matter what, with our without any of them. If they wanted to see her or my brother again, they should leave with her.

Mom's Father gave up everything, his business, his livelihood and his happiness, to follow her to California. At age 65, he was unable to find work in America as an architect or draftsman. He ended up drawing up plans for sidewalks and driveways for Orange County city planning.

A once proud man, my grandfather was reduced to a mere shadow of his former self. He died almost penniless, five years after the death of his wife. His children still bickering over who would take possession of his few remaining things.

Mom told everyone within earshot, that the ONLY reason she left Holland so soon after the war, was to save my brother. She said fruit was in short supply, that my brother had rickets, and needed vitamin C to make him healthy again. California had orange trees and unlimited sunshine, free vitamin D. So she had to go, to save his life.

Mom lied constantly, so just how much of what she said was true, and how much imagined will never be known. Like thousands of other children, my brother developed polio in California. My parents were achingly poor when they arrived in the U.S., they were well off in the Netherlands. The question being, would my brother have developed polio in Holland? While rickets can be easily treated by various means, polio cannot.

Knowing that Mom had lived with an SS officer during the war, I can't help wondering if the real reason she left Holland was to get a fresh start. After all, being branded a collaborator wasn't something one could easily escape or hide from.

Also, after dating so many rich and famous men, why did Mom marry a poor man like my father?

When Dad proposed marriage, why did Mom tell him her little brother Wouter was really her son? When Dad told her he didn't care, and loved her anyway, she told him she was just testing his love for her.

In 1978 my uncle Martin told me that uncle Walt (Wouter) was really my half brother. He said that Mom had gotten knocked-up in her teens. She was removed from school, and sent away with my Grandmother, supposedly to aid her during her confinement. After Wouter was born, he was registered as Amy and Opa's son.

My Mom spoke often about how her Dad removed her from school and sent her away to care for her Mother before she gave birth to Wouter. Both my Mom and her brother Maarten had been born at home. Why would a rich woman, who had never gone into confinement before, suddenly leave town with her teenage daughter? Why wasn't my grandmother attended by her own mother?

When I asked my Mom, why her Mother took her along during confinement, she had no answer. When I asked my Mom how old she was when Walt was born, she paused for a moment and said she'd been 12 years old, which made absolutely no sense. I eventually learned it was also a blatant lie. Wouter was born on 19 May 1937, when my Mother was 16 years old.

Walt Fathered 12 children who I'd always believed were my cousins. The truth is, they're most likely my nieces and nephews. I wasn't able to put all the pieces together until a few years ago, when I started searching for information on my family. I uncovered way too many lies, and the truth about my Dad's family.

In 2012 I sent my Brother a DNA test from ancestry.com. I had taken the same test a few months earlier, and told him I hoped to discover if he and I shared the same Father. For reasons best known to my Brother, after agreeing to take the test, he never followed through.

By the grace of God I've been able to connect with 3rd and 4th cousins related to my Grandmother's side of my family. So odds are in my favor, that Dad was really my biological father. Why Mom put so much energy into making me believe that Dad wasn't my biological father is something I'll never know. Perhaps she had been fooling around at the time, and didn't know herself.

The Bleekrode Family

Figure 1 1936 Leendert Bleekrode,

Five of my Grandmother's relatives were killed in Auschwitz on the 22nd of August 1943. They had been living together in an Amsterdam apartment with a non Jewish family member. A non Jew residing in the Apartment complex reported my Grandmother's family to the Nazi's, who removed the Bleekrodes at gunpoint. Eventually all were transported to Auschwitz and killed on the same day.

My Great Grandfather (Sara's then frail 82-year-old Father) had been living with Sara's family when Nazi soldiers took him away. My Dad had been there when Nazi soldiers removed his Grandfather from their home at gunpoint. Mozes Bleekrode died in a Dutch Concentration camp under Nazi control.

Sara's brother Abraham Bleekrode had been a concert violinist before WWII. During the war, he became a Nazi resistance fighter. His exploits are part of Dutch history. He died in Buchenwald, a little more than a month before the camp was liberated.

My Grandmother Kleintje died in Amsterdam in 1985 (long after the war), she was 96 years old.

Mozes Bleekrode (Sara's Father)

Diamond Cutter

Birth 4 July 1862 in Amsterdam, Netherlands
Death 1 April 1944 in Westerbork Concentration Camp,

Middenveld, Netherlands

Rachel Bleekrode

Birth 24 May 1887 in Amsterdam, Netherlands
Death 22 October 1943 in Auschwitz

daughter: **Rebecca** (by her first husband)

Birth July 1911 in Amsterdam, Netherlands
Death 7 September 1942 in Auschwitz

husband: **Abraham Vogel** (Rachel's second husband)

Birth 14 January 1887 in Amsterdam, Netherlands
Death 22 October 1943 in Auschwitz

Abraham Bleekrode

Violinist, WWII Resistance Fighter

Birth 17 April 1891 in Amsterdam, Netherlands
Death 20 February 1945 in Buchenwald

Abraham's first wife was Maria Petronella Blom, with whom he had two children. His children (Betje and Mozes Bleekrode) went with their Mother after she remarried. Both children of survived the war.

Samuel Bleekrode

Birth 17 June 1893 in Amsterdam, Netherlands
Death 11 February 1944 in Auschwitz

wife: **Vrouwtje Presser**

Birth 28 October 1892 in Amsterdam, Netherlands
Death 11 February 1944 in Auschwitz

son: **Mozes Bleekrode**

Birth 29 September 1924 in Amsterdam, Netherlands
Death 30 September 1942 in Auschwitz

Benjamin Isaäc Bleekrode

Birth 16 May 1895 Amsterdam, Netherlands

wife: **Johanna Daniëlla Garms**

Regina Bleekrode

Birth 27 March 1895 in Amsterdam,
Netherlands
Death 22 October 1943 in <u>Auschwitz</u>

son: **Paul Bleekrode**

Birth 23 August 1923 in Valburg,
Gelderland, Netherlands
Death 22 October 1943 in <u>Auschwitz</u>

Leendert Bleekrode

Birth 3 November 1901 in Amsterdam,
Netherlands
Death unknown

wife: **Esther Jeanette Bleekrode**
Birth date and Death unknown

son: **Ralph Bleekrode**

Birth abt 1938 in Sydney, Australia
Death unknown

It's possible that Leendert survived the
holocaust and didn't die in a
concentration camp. He was traveling
abroad during much of WWII. His wife
Esther was pregnant at the time and gave
birth to their son Ralph in Sydney
Australia.

Hartog Bleekrode

Birth 20 October 1902
Death unknown

Marriage **14 Jan 1931** (Age: 28)
Amsterdam

wife: **Berendina Alida Meeuwig**

Birth date and Death unknown

daughter: **Maria Clasina Bleekrode**

Birth date and Death unknown

Eva Bleekrode

Birth 9 January 1906 in Amsterdam,
Netherlands
Death 22 October 1943 in <u>Auschwitz</u>

Marriage **17 September 1930** (Age:
24) *to* Samuel Gobits
Divorce **23 January 1935** (Age:
29) *from* Samuel Gobits

son: **Robert Sam Gobits**

Birth 29 April 1931 in Amsterdam,
Netherlands
Death 22 October 1943 in <u>Auschwitz</u>

The Silly Yak

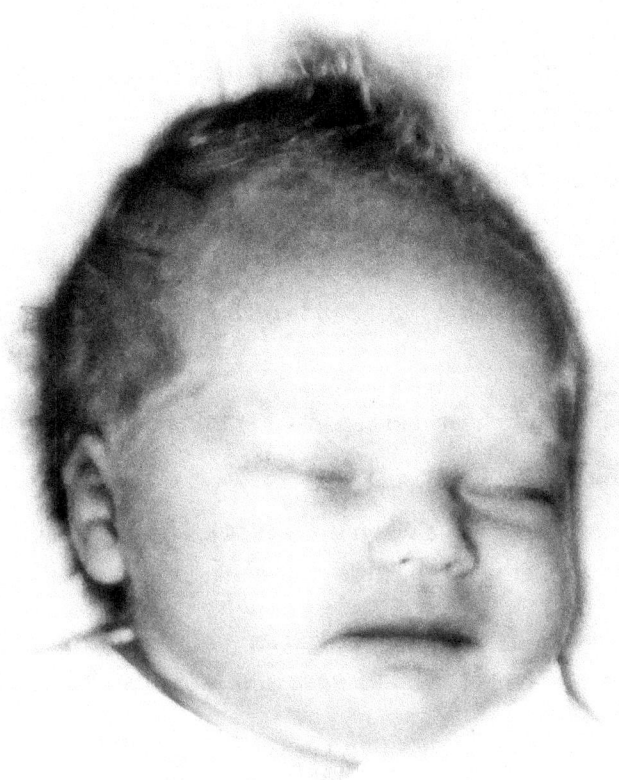

Once upon a time a child was born, unlike any other ... tiny and frail, with bright green eyes and hair the color of spun gold.

She vomited and cried after drinking her mother's milk. So the family labeled her a spoiled, difficult, and ungrateful child. *"Mark my word,"* said the child's Great Aunt sternly, *"this is a sign of bad things to come."*

The little girl's tiny tummy hurt so badly she cried and cried and cried and cried. She cried in the morning, she cried at night, she cried all day long. She cried so much her family grew immune to the sound and simply let her cry alone.

"She'll only cry more if you pick her up." Said the Grandma. The other relatives in the room nodded in agreement.

Snapshots from a Broken Camera

"She'll learn how to be quiet if you leave her alone." Said the Aunt.

But the frail little girl didn't stop crying. So the frail little girl's poor tired Mama shook her until she cried and cried some more. When the little girl went limp and finally stopped crying, Mama placed her in the crib.

The frail little girl into a sickly toddler. The toddler learned to talk. Her tummy had hurt so much and for so long she thought it was normal.

"Mama, I don't feel good." Moaned the little girl.

"There's NOTHING wrong with you." Answered Mama.

The little girl pooed or threw up after meals, and was punished. The little girl grew skinny and pail.

After some meals the little girl's heart beat so fast it scared her. Her Mama called her a big baby.

The little girl learned not to tell Mama when she was sick. She would simply eat, then go to the bathroom and throw up or poo. The little girl remained skinny and pale.

Doctor Stella Davis looked at Mama. "The reason your daughter is anemic and can't gain weight is because she has Celiac Disease and is lactose intolerant Mrs. B."

"Nonsense." Mama answered curtly. "I don't have Celiac Disease, my husband doesn't have Celiac Disease and my Son doesn't have Celiac Disease. No one in my family or my husband's family has ever had Celiac Disease. So my Daughter doesn't have Celiac Disease either."

Rage flooded through Mama. *"Celiac must be an American disease," said Mama haughtily, "because there is no such thing Holland. We are strong healthy Dutch people. In Holland people never get Celiac Disease. Dutch people have eaten lots of bread and cheese for hundreds of years. So my Daughter will eat lots of bread and cheese."*

"You are not a Celiac", said the Mama to the little girl.

"What's a Silly Yak?" asked the little girl.

"NOT YOU!" replied the Mama.

So the little girl grew up thinking it was normal to vomit and have diarrhea and feel sick.

When the little girl's anemia became worse, Mama refused to give her the doctor's anemia medicine. ***"If my daughter needs iron, why buy expensive baby pills when I can get something stronger with more iron?"*** So Mama gave the little girl Grandma's Geritol, which made her diarrhea and tummy ache much much worse.

I Never Could Eat a Horse

"Geef haar paardenvlees" (Feed her horse meat) said Grandma.

The little girl cried and threw up when they forced her to eat horse meat. The almost raw, red bloody meat scared her, and she cried for the horse. ***"Mama, please don't make me eat a dead horsey."***

"Rot Kind (rotten child), said Mama while holding the little girl down. "I paid good money for this meat." Holding up a piece of bloody red meat.) Eat it or I'll spank you."

Snapshots from a Broken Camera

"No!" cried the little girl.

"Rot Kind!" scolded Grandma, wagging her long manicured finger.

"Rot Kind!" hissed Mama, who then spanked the little girl until she cried.

So the little girl took double doses of her Grandmother's Geritol and ate all the bloody red meat (cooked in butter) and the nearly raw egg (also cooked in butter) and the big glass of whole raw milk, and then vomited and pooed all afternoon.

"Stupid selfish girl," said Mama with an angry scowl, "you're making yourself sick." The frail little girl looked up from the toilet, then bent over and vomited again. "Stop that right now!" Demanded Mama.

Mama walked into the living room and shrugged. Everyone in the house walked up to Mama. One by one they showered her with hugs and kisses.

"You poor dear girl, what a horrible nightmare of a child you have." said the Great Aunt. Everyone nodded. "An ordeal." Said the Aunt. "A trial." Said the Grandmother.

Mama wiped the tears from her eyes and looked toward her loving family. "But she's so beautiful and I love her very much, can she be saved? What must I do?"

"We will help, but you must be strong, or your daughter will always be a problem child." Answered Mama's family.

Hugging her throbbing tummy, the little girl curled up on the floor in front of the toilet and whimpered softly, she had just messed her pants. Shivering and afraid, she knew Mama would be mad when she found out.

I'm sure you've figured out by now the little girl in this story is me.

I was born with various food and medication allergies. Allergies which went undiagnosed and untreated until I was in my mid 40s.

February 1966
Santa Ana, California

My Dad and Brother got into a horrible fight today.

My brother was a senior in high school. For years I'd been hearing about how my brother had been using Dad's camera to take pictures for his high school paper. Dick borrowed Dad's cameras all the time. He took care of them, cleaned them and made sure they were in great shape.

Unfortunately today Dad had been at work, and there was no one to ask. So my brother simply borrowed the Camera, like he had a million times before. Thinking it would be OK, Dick used the camera to take pictures today.

Only it wasn't OK. Upon learning my brother had used his camera without asking, Dad went insane with anger. Dad screamed at my brother for what seemed like hours. His hands clinched at his side, my brother remained silent and stony faced during the entire ordeal.

At some point Mom got between my brother and my Dad. She told my Dad to calm down and pick up some burgers. Still red faced with anger, Dad stomped noisily out of the house and drove off in his VW.

Mom was talking quickly to my brother making excuses for my Dad. Suddenly my quiet Brother, who had NEVER talked back, was shouting in my Mother's face. *"You know I take better care of Dad's cameras then he does. I'm tired of his bullshit, and I'm tired of yours."*

Enough Mom ENOUGH!

Mom grabbed hold of her chest. My brother flew into a rage. *"Go ahead, GET SICK LIKE YOU ALWAYS DO."* Mom leaned against the wall of my brother's bedroom, looking at my brother pleadingly, sadly, tears welling in her eyes. My Brother returned her questioning gaze with pure unadulterated hatred.

Still looking at my brother, Mom slowly slid down onto the floor. Now hugging herself, Mom began howling like a wounded animal. *"I HOPE YOU DIE!"* Dick screamed while hammering his fist against the wall.

Snapshots from a Broken Camera

Dick pulled his fist back and slammed it so hard against the wall that it broke through. Pieces drywall were raining down on Mom. Her head looked as if it were covered in snow. Dick unclenched his fist and ran out of the house.

I stood in the doorway looking at my Mom's now ashen face, listening to her moaning like some sort of wounded animal. I tried talking to her, and she didn't respond. When I tried touching her she pushed me away, slid face down onto the ground and continued moaning.

By the time Dad came home Mom was still moaning and crying hysterically on the floor of my brother's room. The sound of it terrified me. Dad got Mom up and took her to their bedroom. He got her a glass of water and some Valium … she threw both across the room.

I went in my room and closed my door.

Doctor Doctor Help Me Doctor

30 minutes later the door bell rang. Dad had called the doctor. I heard footsteps in the hallway, followed by voices in my parent's bedroom.

"Breathe slowly Mrs. Barkemeijer," I heard doctor Edward's calm voice coming from my parent's bedroom. *"Try to relax Nel. You're fine."*

"I AM NOT fine … I'm having a heart attack!"

"You're fine Nel, you're not having a heart attack." The doctor was talking to my Dad now, in the hallway. *"Dick, do you have a paper bag I can use?"* *"Sure Doctor Edwards, sure."*

It's in the Bag

A few minutes later my Mom was screaming on the top of her lungs. *"Get that God damned bag I away from me! Do you think I'm an idiot? Do you think I don't know what you're trying to do?"*

Doctor Edwards stood his ground. *"Calm down Nel and try breathing in the bag, it will help slow down your heart rate."*

"You think I'm some hysterical idiot and you want me to believe that there's nothing wrong with me. I'm NOT HYPERVENTILATING! I'm having a heart attack! YOU THINK I DON'T KNOW WHEN I'M HAVING A HEART ATTACK?! My mother died of a heart attack. Now I'm having a heart attack and will die if I don't get to a hospital!"

The sound of my Mother's screams terrified me. She'd said she was dying. I couldn't stop shaking. My Mom was dying in the next room and there was nothing I could do.

I heard a car pulling up in our driveway. I could see red lights flashing against my window. I stood up on my bed and pulled back the curtain. A long white ambulance was parking there. I ran into my bathroom and vomited. After washing my face I opened my bedroom door and walked to my parent's room.

Mom was lying on the bed with her hands clutching her chest. *"Mom?"* I asked softly, wanting to comfort her. *"GET HER OUT GET HER AWAY FROM ME!!!"* She screamed while waving me away. *"I need to get in the ambulance NOW ... before I DROP DEAD!"*

Dr Edwards came over and gave me a hug. *"Your Mom's fine Honey."* he whispered in my ear. *"There's nothing wrong with her, she's just scared."*

Mom continued screaming *"Doesn't ANYONE see I'm having a heart attack?"*

Dr Edwards squeezed my hand and kissed me on the forehead. *"Honey you don't need to hear this. Why don't you go into your room and turn on the radio."* He motioned to my Dad and pointed to my room. Dad didn't respond or move from my Mom's side.

A big metal gurney was in our living room along with two men in white suits. I slowly backed into my room just as the men were helping Mom onto the gurney. I sat on my bed and someone slammed my bedroom door shut. I could hear Doctor Edwards talking to someone on the kitchen phone. It sounded like he was talking to someone at a hospital.

I heard cars starting up in the driveway. Dozens of people were standing outside the front of our house. The red lights blinked on and off and people cleared away from the driveway. The doctor drove off, the ambulance behind him ... my Dad following them all. My Mom was dying and I was home alone for the only second time in my life. The last time I was home alone I was raped.

Eleanor Rigby

> *"Ah, look at all the lonely people*
> *Ah, look at all the lonely people"*

A couple of years prior, almost to the day, Amy (my grandmother) had gone to the hospital and never returned. Now Mom was on her way to the hospital to die.

Snapshots from a Broken Camera

"Eleanor Rigby died in the church and was buried along with her name
Nobody came"

The sound Paul McCartney's voice, so pure, so familiar, made my head spin. The lyrics tugged at my soul. I started to cry.

"Father McKenzie wiping the dirt from his hands as he walks from the grave
No one was saved"

No one, not my Dad, not my Mom, NO ONE, bothered to checked on me or thought to send over someone to stay with me. Everyone just got in their cars and left. I didn't know where anyone had gone, or how long I'd be home alone. I was only 10 years old.

Home alone for an eternity, I watched the sun circle the earth. I followed the morning shadows as they danced along the front of the house and my bedroom window to our backyard and onto the afternoon.

The outside sky went from a bright Oregon blue to soft gold to pink to royal blue and black. I watched the night shadows rise up and swallow my bedroom window. When the house was shrouded in darkness I watched a million stars pop up and dot the sky.

Looking out my bedroom window I saw the moon making a slow lazy circle in the night sky. I watched cars come and go from our neighbor's homes. I saw mothers and fathers in suits, workman's clothing and uniforms head into the homes around me.

I heard the sounds of canned television laughter wafting from a dozen homes. I smelled dinners served up to happy families, and imagined loving mothers hugging their children.

I was a ghost no one could see. The only thing I could touch was my window. The things I saw outside belonged in the living world, I did not. Eleanor Rigby had died, and so had I.

No adults were home to turn on the house lights, or the porch light, or the patio light. Too afraid to move, too terrified to walk through the now dark house, I lay shivering on my bed. It had been dark for hours before I learned my Mom was still alive.

Mom returned home with swollen tear streaked eyes, heavily sedated and barely able to walk. I was invisible. Dad took Mom straight to bed. When I got up to check on her she was staring blankly at the ceiling. I was invisible.

When I checked on Dad he was in the kitchen eating one of the now cold hamburgers he had purchased earlier in the day. ***"I'm hungry too Dad"***, I thought to myself, before realizing I was invisible or dead and he couldn't see me.

Later, much later, when my brother returned to the house, he went from the front door directly to his room. He and I were both invisible. Eleanor Rigby was playing on the radio when he came home, as it had been off and on all that day.

Whenever I hear Eleanor Rigby, I'm always transported back to the same day. A day in 1966, when my world turned upside down, and I found myself alone.

"All the lonely people
Where do they all come from?
All the lonely people
Where do they all belong?"

1 **Authors: Lennon, McCartney; Lead vocal: McCartney 1966**

In the Blink of an Eye

Friday - May 29 1970
Santa Ana, California
5:45PM

The Beginning of Memorial Day Weekend

My Mom and I were on our way home from South Coast Plaza. We'd been there since a little after 10am. My Dad had invited "his girls" out to lunch at Kaplan's Deli. A Sort'a Kind'a big deal this luncheon ... more for what it could have meant ... than what eventually transpired.

The previous 12 months had seen so much sadness and death. My Mother's Dad (Opa to me) died on December 7th 1969. My Mom had taken the news of my Brother's marriage as badly as she had her father's death. All "her" dreams for him started dying the day he left home, and she was shattered to bits when he later married. Small wonder neither my brother and his wife wanted contact with my Mom.

Dad went to Amsterdam that year, like always, and I was left home alone with Mom. After school Mom took me to Fountain Convalescent Hospital, where Opa was. During the week, visited every day. On weekends and Holidays my Mom and I were there all day. After I visited Opa I went from room to room to room visiting people. I also played piano for anyone who wanted to listen. On movie days I watched MGM musicals with the residents.

In September of 1969 when Opa's health began failing, my Mom more or less vanished into a dark and inaccessible place. She became blind to the needs of almost everyone but her Father. While most of Opa's needs were attended to by nurses, Mom was there every day and helped cared for him as well.

Even at the best of times Mom was a hard, brittle, and self absorbed individual. Her tenuous hold on sanity was thrown into the abyss by her Father's impending death. When my cat took ill (blocked bladder) I begged for someone to take him in to the Vet. My Mom slapped me silly and told me "no one has time for a god damned cat". My cat Pussy Willow and my love for him were just so much collateral damage.

Life at home was so cold harsh I wished and prayed that God would let me die. I lost count of how many nights I cried myself to sleep.

Unable to get help for my cat, and not knowing what I could do, I was forced to watch Pussy Willow endure a slow and agonizing death. I couldn't even touch him without causing him pain. He died bloated twice his normal size, writhing in pain. The memories of that time triggered years of nightmares. Those days haunt me to this day.

No Christmas that year … not really … not that it mattered. I was living alone by then, surrounded by ghosts both living and dead … invisible to all. All the people Mom really cared about were gone. Her Dad had just died, her Mom died five years prior, and my newly married Brother was as good as dead in her mind. She mourned them all with a single minded vengeance that seemed horrifying to my young mind.

Alone in Vancouver

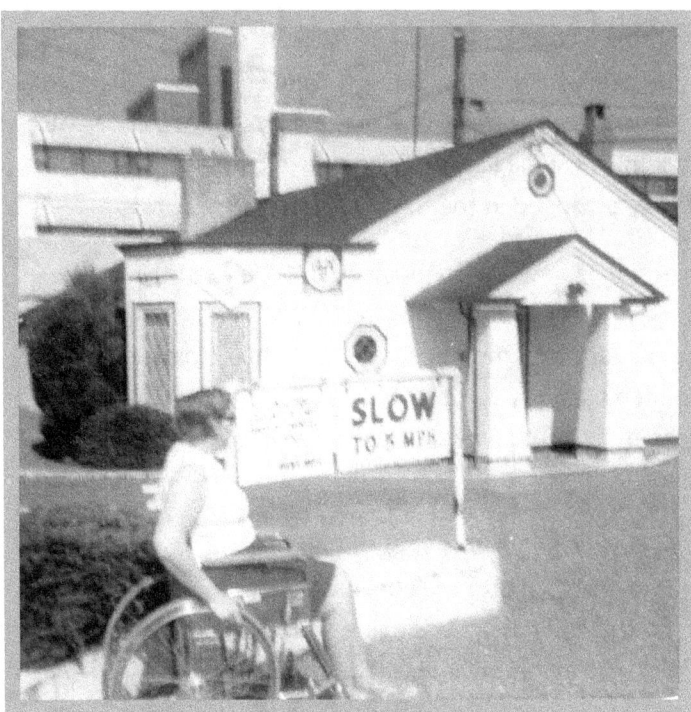

Mom and I spent a week in the Astor Hotel (tall building in the background of the photo), then moved into a cheap Motel (with monthly rates) next door to the Astor. We slept together in a tiny fold out sofa.

I spent the summer of 1970 pushing my Mom around Vancouver in a wheelchair, barely able to walk myself. I bought the groceries, cooked, and did laundry in the bathtub. When we ran out of toilet paper we tore up my Mom's newspaper and used it.

I remember walking and down Kingsway by myself when my Mom was in too much pain to go out. My shoes didn't fit, (my Mom had told me my feet were too big and that no one made shoes in my size). As a result I my feet were in almost constant pain. I walked barefoot whenever possible. It wasn't until I was an adult and able to purchase my own shoes I learned they manufactured shoes in size 10 and over. By then it was too late and my feet had suffered permanent damage.

Snapshots from a Broken Camera

Five days a week my Dad was more like a residual ghost than a living person. Dad got up at 7am, lit a cigarette coughed and hacked, shaved, smoked some more, dressed, smoked some more, coughed and hacked some more, ate, smoked some more, and still smoking, drove off to work. When he returned home at 6pm, he smoked and talked with my mother for hours. Dad continued smoking and taking to Mom throughout dinner, and then watched television on the recliner until 11:30pm. I wasn't really there to either of my parents

A few years earlier, before my brother moved from home, when things were still semi-normal ... as normal as things ever were in my home. I made the decision to get baptized. Pam Fancher, my best friend, introduced me to her church. Her parents had been taking me to church with them. Nothing unusual about that, various neighbors had been taking me to church for as long as I could remember. It got me out of my Mom's hair on Sundays.

I lived for the Sundays I was able to attend "my" church. I loved Mrs. Lambeth ("Dusty" to other parishioners), our Pastor Dr Gerald Bash, and Jack Coleman the choir director. I loved going into the sanctuary to sing, the sound of the great organ, the silky feel of a choir rob against my skin. The sanctuary was a mystical magical place to me. A place where our children's voices could sound as if they belonged in the Mormon tabernacle.

Jack Coleman wasn't a phony, something I knew all too much about. He lived the love of God he was constantly telling us about. He was warm and kind and caring. I couldn't sing back then, too many strep throats had damaged my voice. Not that I had a bad voice, I couldn't always control what it sounded like. My voice would pop up and hit strange raspy notes, go sour, or worse yet die altogether. But I was still welcomed into the choir. All God's children were welcome.

Jack taught me, taught us all, how to sing. One day my voice found me, and I began to sing, really sing. I remember hearing my voice go out into the cool sanctuary air, sounding pure and true. Jack Coleman looked at me and smiled. I was singing and crying and thanking God for allowing me a place in his home. Two days later ... when the call was given ... I walked forward to accept.

Church was OK with my family, but baptism was something to be scorned. After I mentioned it became a target. It was as if someone tacked a bull's eye on my forehead. My Dad heckled me for weeks. I remember making the mistake of coming to the kitchen table with my new bible and being forced to listen to my Dad singing the benediction "Holy Holy Holy" in a taunting voice. My brother sat and watched and said nothing. My Mom said nothing. I felt so alone and lost I pulled even further away from my family.

At church people acted normal, seemed to love one and other, and treated me like I was really there. Now that Opa was dying I only went to Church when someone was willing to take me. Basically this meant I went when Pam Fancher's Dad took me with them. Which by then wasn't all the time, because both Pam and I were in the Children's choir.

The problem was the Children's choir sang at first service and we had to be there at 7am to warm up and practice. Suffice it to say I missed a lot of services and choir rehearsals. I remember trying to wake up my Mom so I could get to church. She picked up an aluminum cup she kept on her nightstand, threw it at me, and told me to leave her the hell alone.

In order for me to get baptized, the church required me to get a permission slip signed by one of my parents. I went to see Dr Bash with my Mom. When we left I learned my Mom (who had NEVER attended my church) was getting baptized with me! I had mixed feelings.

I had wanted my baptism to be private. I had wanted the moment to be about me spending quiet time with God. It felt like Mom was making MY baptism all about her.

Suddenly my Dad was attending church with my Mom. He was famous for his loud singing voice and for falling asleep in the back pews. Sometimes we'd go to Bob's Big Boy for breakfast after church. Sometimes Pam joined us.

Years later, when I was grown, and attending another church, my Dad had heard I wanted a copy of the "Lamsa Bible". Dr Lamsa had been given permission to read and translate the "lost sea scrolls". I was interested in seeing the differences between the traditional bible and Dr Lamsa's. A few days later my Dad handed me a copy, which he signed for me. I was touched that he had thought of me. I still own it.

After Opa died, Mom told the neighbors she'd put a tree up for Dad and me. Not true, because we weren't really alive to her. Mom put up a Christmas tree covered with blue ornaments and tinsel, to honor her Dad's memory.

Mom came down with the Swine flu a few days after her Dad died. It eventually progressed to pneumonia. Dad never stayed away from work. He pulled me from school and told to take care of my Mom. I'd missed a lot of school that year. I was sick a lot and had always missed a lot of school. School was important for my brother, not a girl like me.

By then I had begun letting paper, clothing and trash pile up throughout my bedroom. I felt safer on the floor surrounded by clutter and trash than I did anyplace else. I remember lying on the ground trying to wish myself invisible so I could vanish inside the trash ... which is what I felt like.

Snapshots from a Broken Camera

Memorial Day - May 29, 1970 - was to have been special - Dad was taking Mom and me to lunch. Something he'd never done before. More than anything else ::: I longed for it to be special. I cleaned my room, removed the trash, washed my clothing and hoped. "What can it mean ... what can it mean?" My Mom had asked me for days. "He's going to take us on Vacation with him to Holland!" I hoped whatever Dad had to tell us would be magical.

Jack Coleman was in Hawaii with the Children's Choir, my choir. Mom had said no to my going with them to perform. She said they couldn't afford it and wouldn't have agreed to let me go even if they could. Her words were like salt on an open wound. "Hawaii is too far away and too dangerous, you could get raped and murdered or end up pregnant." Mom had said. Her standard arguments against anything I wanted to do. Rape, murder, pregnancy.

Every year my Dad went to Holland to see his folks. Every year my Mom hoped and prayed he would take us (my family) with him. Dad went because he loved his parents and my Mom had forced him to immigrate to America ... something he never let her forget. He became a travel agent so he'd be able to travel cheap even though we were poor.

When I was little I didn't understand why he left. Today, with all the excitement of lunch I finally believed he was going to take us with him. I didn't mind missing Hawaii.

Dad dropped the bomb just after eating lunch. Dad chose the perfect day and perfect spot ... too many people for Mom to make a scene. On this Friday before Memorial Day, Kaplan's Deli was so jammed full of people they had opened their back dining area.

Dad threw his airline tickets on the table. He was leaving in a few weeks ... alone.

Mom was staring at Dad, silently watching him as he stood up and grabbed his wallet. "See you girls tonight. Glad we had lunch together. Let's do it again when I get back from Amsterdam." Then he picked up his tickets and walked away.

There was no mistaking Dad's walk. His stride was like a soldier's, his back upright and straight, his feet clomp clomp clomping heavily on the floor with a military cadence.

I watched my scoop of chocolate ice cream turning into mush, the sound of my Dad's feet drumming in my ear. Mom looked right through me and into the wall. She'd fallen back into the dark place she'd been residing for the last two years and I was invisible again.

My Mom, the Mom I used to know, died that Friday afternoon, and I never really saw her again. I didn't know this person sitting next to me at Kaplan's. The stranger was crying, silently dabbing at tears between long drags on countless cigarettes.

The Mom I knew, my Mom, was always involved, always on the go, always in charge. A stranger had replaced my Mom and taken up permanent residence in our booth. It seemed as if she were content to sit in Kaplan's forever, swathed in tobacco smoke.

After 30 minutes, the hostess came to our both and politely told the stranger to leave ... they were too crowded and needed the seating. The stranger looked past the hostess with blank red rimmed eyes and didn't move. "I'll give you and your daughter a moment miss," said the hostess quietly "then you both need to leave."

The stranger slowly tossed her smoldering cigarette inside my Mom's half empty coffee cup, gathered my Mom's things and rose to leave. The stranger exited Kaplan's with me following behind.

When we exited Kaplan's the stranger walked over to the fountain just outside, sat down on a bench, put her gloves in her purse and removed her high heels. Appearances were EVERYTHING to my Mom. She never went out without nylons, high heels, makeup and gloves. The dead eyed stranger sitting next to me didn't care.

The stranger walked up and down the lower level of South Coast Plaza for close to 4 hours. She walked shoeless between Sears and May Company, past the Galleon, past the carousel, past the food court and beauty salons and a dozen other stores. I followed her for a while, but eventually wandered off by myself, walking around the mall and looking at different stores, while keeping an eye on my Mom.

At 5:30pm PT we found ourselves inside Sears. The stranger was staring at me. She looked up and said "You father will be home soon, we need to leave." The stranger sat down on a bench and returned Mom's trademark stiletto shoes to her feet. Our car was just outside. We walked out of Sears together.

Memorial Day traffic was insane. It looked as if the regular 10 minute drive to our house would take close to an hour. I'd never seen so many cars on the street. By the time we reached the intersection of Bristol and McFadden, traffic was at a near standstill.

Mom turned onto McFadden and eased over to the far right lane. The light on Pacific had just turned yellow when a car suddenly veered in our path ... cutting us off and racing past the intersection to avoid the red light. I remember looking at my Mom and saying "that was close".

Suddenly, out of the corner of my eye, I noticed a car coming at us from across the street. We were at a full stop, sandwiched between a million cars, with no place to go.

Snapshots from a Broken Camera

As if in a dream, I watched the car to our left back up into the left suicide lane in reverse and keep on going. As if in a dream, I watched the other car racing towards us through the break in traffic. As if in a dream, I watched our two cars collide.

My Mom placed her arm against me to shield me from impact. When she touched me ... time seemed to stop ... and the world lost sync with the laws of physics. Everything around me was moving in slow motion. I heard the sound of groaning metal and breaking glass and felt myself floating gently around the inside of the car. Mom didn't believe in seat belts.

My head was slowly gliding towards the right passenger car door ::: "my" door. I raised my arms and easily pushed myself away. The car was gliding backward now. Amazed, I felt my body rising from my seat. I watched my feet rise up and touch the dashboard. I raised my arms again and pushed against the hood of the car. An instant later my body was rammed down onto the floor of the car.

When the car came to a stop, my rump was on the floor, my feet up against the windshield, my knees up near my face, and my head was resting against my seat. I was covered in broken glass.

After what seemed like an eternity of jarring noise, the sudden silence was disorienting. To my left was my Mom. I could see that her feet had disappeared beneath the car's floor and were now embedded where the brake pedal had been. Her face was a ghastly shade of pale ashen grey ... her nose was broken and bloody, her lips blue ... a slender ribbon of blood oozed from her right ear.

She'd broken the steering column on impact. Her neck was draped over the steering wheel in an odd angle. She wasn't breathing. I shook her and she fell over limp next to me on the seat, her feet still embedded in the floor of the car. She took in a single deep breath and color began returning to her blue grey lips.

My car door was half open. I can still hear the strange creaking sound the door made as I pushed it open. I stood up and viewed the carnage surrounding us. Our car, and the car that hit us, had merged into a single misshapen pile of fractured glass and smoldering metal.

I could see a pair of legs sticking up in the back seat of the other car ::: the driver. Glass was everywhere. I saw a man's head encased in the cracked and fissured remains of what had been the front windshield of the other car. I watched the man twist and pull his head until it was free. He looked at me in tears and asked if I was OK. I didn't know.

The driver ::: I was later told he was a drug addict and alcoholic ::: had just been released from jail earlier that morning. He and his companion had been partying all day.

My Mom suffered multiple cuts and bruises, soft tissue damage, a fractured skull, broken nose, broken ribs, broken feet and a brain contusion. She was in a coma for 8 days afterward. I tore all the muscles on my left side, fractured countless teeth, suffered multiple cuts and bruises, a brain contusion, soft tissue damage to my left side, and a dislocated jaw.

Mom regained consciousness briefly in the Ambulance. She asked me what happened. I told her we'd been in a car accident. Her response was a dull uninterested "Oh." She told me to call Steve when I got to a phone. Amazingly she knew his number by heart.

I was astonished that she wanted me to call Steve, her x-lover, the man who molested me throughout my childhood. The man who eventually raped me, strangled me and left me for dead. The man she refused to believe had ever hurt me in any way. "You dreamed it." was her standard reply.

I picked up my purse and scribbled Steve's phone number on a notepad, and then passed out while returning the notepad to my purse.

I woke up in the hospital while someone was cutting off my clothes. I was so big and tall the people working on me assumed I was an adult. When I tried to make them stop cutting my clothes, they held me down and told me to stop acting like a child. As they tugged on a hospital gown, the room faded back into grey.

I regained consciousness on a cold hard X-Ray table, screaming in pain. Lay still ... lay still ... this will go quickly if you lay still. The room turned spun and then turned gray when the technician shoved a foam wedge against my back.

I woke up again on a gurney inside a big room filled with at least a half dozen strange women. My Mom was in bed next to me, laying strangely still. Her makeup was gone and her face was covered with bruises. "ONE ... TWO ... THREE" suddenly I was lifted off the gurney and onto a bed. Someone handed me a plastic box. "If you need anything push this." Suddenly everyone was gone, the door was shut, and it was pitch dark.

In a wild panic I clutched the box and began frantically pushing buttons. A television on the other side of the room fluttered to life. I could see my Mom's face in the light. My panic started to fade. The woman below the television was calling out. "Nurse ... nurse .... will you PLEASE come here."

Snapshots from a Broken Camera

Five minutes later a nurse came in, bent over to hear the woman speak, then stood up and turned off the television. "Sorry about that. Don't know how the television came on. Get some sleep now."

The complete darkness terrified me, always had. Bad things happened to me at night. My panic returned. I grabbed the plastic box the nurse had handed to me and pushed the buttons again. Suddenly a voice came out of the box. "Can I help you?" Startled, I whispered "I'm scared". "I can't hear you" replied the box. I began to cry.

A tall dark haired woman came to my bed and asked me what was wrong. I told her I was afraid of the dark and she laughed. "You can't have the television on all night, and I can't keep the door open." Then she left.

The woman returned with a hypodermic syringe. I asked what she was going to do. "Give you something to help you sleep." She drove the needle into my arm as I was begging her not to. afterward I lay unconscious for two days. (After my accident, when I saw my pediatrician she said the nurse nearly killed me.)

I don't remember how many weeks had passed when my Dad took me home from the hospital. All I remember is that he came and got me after work. My Dad drove an old beige VW with a stick. My Dad drove fast.

The evening Dad took me home, I screamed every time he accelerated or turned left into rush hour traffic. He yelled and scowled at me … cigarette jutting from his mouth … told me to shut up and stop being a baby. So I closed my eyes, tried not to breathe in the smoke, and gripped the seat of his car. I shook and cried for the remainder of the trip.

My entire left side was an ugly shade of deep purple and blue. Dad drove me around so I could to show my bruises his friends. A dozen times he instructed me to lift my top and lower my pants just enough to let them see. I was self conscious but he insisted. The room was spinning and I could barely stand, but he couldn't tell. Everyone stared and commented how sore my bruises looked. No one once asked me how I felt, or if I needed to sit down.

When Dad and I got home the refrigerator was almost empty, there was no food on the stove, no milk to drink. The sink was piled full of dirty dishes. My room was so clean I almost didn't recognize it. I'd forgotten, hoping for magic, I'd cleaned it up weeks ago. The room next to mine, my brother's old room, later my grandfather's room (now used for storage) was full of boxes and other odds and ends my Mom had placed there.

I lay down on my bed and thought about the choir and my friends in Hawaii and wished I was with them. I cried myself to sleep ::: too tired and too weak and too sore to undress.

That night my Dad had one grand mal seizure after another. Afterwards, he roamed the house in a daze crying out in Dutch for his "Mama". When he stumbled into my room wearing nothing but urine soaked underpants, I ran into my bathroom and locked the door.

I lay down on the hard cold linoleum floor of my bathroom, my head under the sink and my feet against the toilet. When my Dad kept banging on my bathroom door I cupped my ears and prayed that God would take me, let me die. I prayed until I fell asleep, not waking up until the morning light was shining in through my bathroom window.

There were no happy endings that year ... or the years that followed. I lived in a sort of vacuum ... a place with little warmth or care. No one came to protect me, help me or save me. I was alone in a way no child should ever be.

The first day back to High school I told my physical education teacher that I'd been in a car accident and wouldn't be able to do P.E. for a while. She called me a liar and a looser.

I'd always been sick and missed a lot of school. My new gym teacher thought I'd been truant, and was cutting class. She thought I was fat and lazy and lord knows what else. She didn't know my family, the hell I was living in, and had never believed me when I told her my periods (primary dysmenorrhea) were too painful and too bloody for me to swim.

"You shouldn't listen the stories told to you by your Mom. Painful menstruation is a myth propagated by ignorant uneducated women who don't know any better. Modern women don't have bad periods. Modern women know better. So put on your swimsuit and get into the pool." She tossed me a tampon. "Put this in and you'll be fine."

Embarrassed by the teacher's tirade, embarrassed by my body ... I locked myself into a bathroom stall and undressed. I tried as best I could to stop the blood from running down my legs. I cleaned myself up, inserted the tampon (my first), and pulled up my school issued swim suit. When I entered the pool clouds of translucent red surrounded me, then vanished. Interestingly my period eventually stopped while I was in the water, only to return two fold when I got exited the pool.

Today her distrust was no different. Despite a doctor's note, my gym teacher said she didn't believe me and ordered me to strip in front of the class so she could see for herself. If I didn't look bruised she was going to force me to suit for P.E. Too sore and too weary to voice any objections, I complied.

Snapshots from a Broken Camera

I had to struggle to pull down my pants and lift my top over my head. I remember standing half naked in front of everyone and asking if she believed me now. Bruises covered my entire left side. My gym teacher motioned for me to get dressed and go to the nurse's office. I never spoke to her again.

After Mom came home from the hospital she couldn't walk. She moved around the house in a wheelchair, shuffling the chair forward with her hands and feet. I could barely get myself up from bed or a chair. Not knowing how to cook anything beyond fried eggs and bacon … Dad brought home McDonald burgers to keep us fed. When Mom could make the trip we ate at Thrifty's coffee shop.

Dad canceled his trip to Amsterdam, and for a while it looked as if things were better between Mom and Dad. The hospital sent a nice black woman to the house to fix food and help around the house for a few weeks. One of my Mom's friends came and took us to physical therapy each day. My church set up some people to pick me up from school and watch me until my Dad came to take me home. I missed my Jr High graduation. Mom called it "a pointless waste of time and money".

In July Mom and Dad had a huge fight. Dad had just told her he was going to Holland. He said "We were healing up now, and could take care of ourselves". Mom had other ideas. Mom canceled our physical therapy, canceled church assistance, and canceled our visiting nurse.

She booked two tickets to Canada and told me we were going to stay with "Uncle" Steve. She didn't know Steve had taken up with another woman. A woman with young children he could molest.

Steve picked us up from the airport, so Naturally Mom was able to talk him into visiting. He'd stop by often to take Mom out. "For a Drink", said my Mom ... a woman who hardly drank. Mom left me to watch TV alone or do "whatever", while she drove off with Steve.

My Mom, the woman who NEVER let me go places alone, sleep over at my friends homes, join traveling choirs, orchestras and church groups, because she was afraid I'd get knocked up, be raped, molested, left for dead. The same Mom felt free to leave me alone in British Columbia, our special magical place. Because Canada was safe, no one was ever molested or killed in Canada. So she left me alone for hours while she went for drinks with Steve.

Stephan Takatch, the man who molested me over and, from age 6 until years later when he raped me and the choked me and left me for dead. Stephan, the man Mom forced me to kiss and apologize to for lying and telling her he had "touched me, down there".

From that moment on Steve owned me, because my Mom believed HIM, not me. So I endured the unendurable throughout my childhood. Until finally, blessedly, Steve raped and almost killed me. After he believed I was dead, he finally left me alone.

After Steve raped me and left me for dead, he got into his car and kept driving until he arrived in Canada, where he stayed until he died. Only Steve's story, the story he told my Mom, was that he'd finally had it with his wife. My Mom was ecstatic, and began visiting him in Canada. Never going alone, and always taking along family, so no one ever knew.

When Steve picked us up at the airport and he told me "this is where I put little' lee (he couldn't pronounce little) girls who tell". He was pointing to a patch of ground from the freeway. He looked at me with red rimmed eyes from the rear view mirror. The he reached over into the back seat, grabbed my hand and squeezed hard. "You hear me little' lee girl?"

Like always, Mom never heard or saw anything Steve did, other than what she wanted to see. He was HER lover, so obviously there was no way someone SHE was with would be sexually attracted to her child. When I tried to tell my Mom things he was doing she suddenly became deaf dumb and blind. "You dreamt it." or "You imagined it" were her standard responses to ANYTHING I said she hadn't wanted to hear.

When Mom went out with Steve I would walk up and down the sidewalk near our motel. Walking on Kingsway I saw parents with their children, families and people doing things together. I wept when I saw church signs inviting parents to bring their children in for summer day camp. Life went on around me. No one ever noticed my tears. No one ever noticed my bruises. No one ever offer assistance. No one.

Snapshots from a Broken Camera

When I pushed my Mom around Vancouver, B.C., in her wheelchair, people were always walking up to her. They would ask what had happened, how she felt and if she would walk again. She would recount the story of my evil thoughtless father and how he had always chosen trips to Holland over her. Women would cry while listening, men would shake their heads in amazement and offer to buy her drinks. Occasionally someone would pat me on the head, or tell me how lucky I was to have such a special Mother. Mostly I was invisible. I was Mom's servant, her property, her bitch.

I turned 15 in Canada the year of the accident. No gifts, no phone calls from Dad or my Brother. On my birthday, the girls at the Astor put a candle on a cupcake and sang to me. That evening Mom and I each ate a small can of Dinty Moore Stew (a special treat) in our tiny hotel room. As always, I spent the day caring for my Mom. When we went to bed on our small pull out sofa bed, Mom hugged me and said I was her special angel.

We returned home late August, a few days after my Dad had left for Amsterdam.

The house was filthy. Dust was everywhere. The place stank of dirty socks, cigarette smoke and tobacco. The sink was full of mold and maggot encrusted dishes, and the hampers were overflowing with Dad's soiled clothing.

Other than a half empty bag of peanut MnM's (Dad's favorite), some mayonnaise, a partial loaf of Wonder bread, and two cans of Coke (also Dad's favorite), the refrigerator was empty. I found cans of frozen orange juice in the freezer, boxes of instant potatoes and cans of tuna in the cupboard. I fixed tuna and mashed potatoes (I called them Tuna sundaes) and served them with cold glasses orange juice ... until we ran out.

With little food remaining in the house, Mom called my brother every day for over a week, begging him to bring over some food. In a way he was right to ignore her calls. Mom could easily have called one of the neighbors, the church, or any number of friends. But Mom wasn't really worried about our lack of food, what she wanted was to see my brother. Only I didn't know that. So when we had no more food, and no one came to bring any, I offered to go to the store myself.

I took my bike to the grocery store and picked up a bag of food. Unfortunately the muscles on my left side were still too weak. On the way home the bag I was carrying shifted and I lost control of my bike. I ended up on the street with broken bottles and damaged food. I returned home bloody and disheartened. At which point my Mom quickly called my Brother to tell him what had just happened to me. My brother drove over the next day, angry and upset. He dropped off a bag of food and left.

I returned to high school in the fall of 1970, friendless, alone and in constant pain. Over the summer I had gone from a size 14 to a size 24. I was heckled for my size, the way I walked and the way I looked.

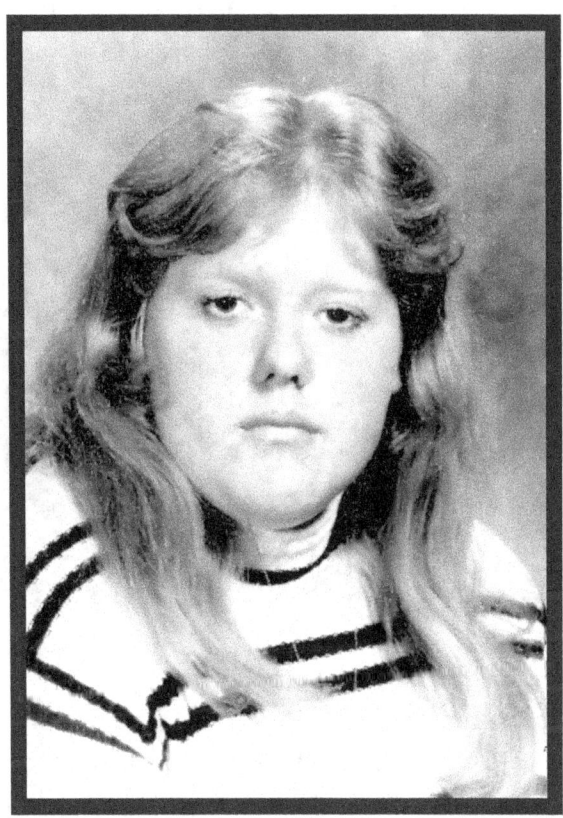

1970 - High school photo take when I was 15

Snapshots from a Broken Camera

Stephan Takatch

Mom's many trips to Canada had never been for anyone but her. This time was no different. I was along so she could maintain the facade of a caring Mother taking a trip with her Daughter. The year before that she had taken my friend Pam along with us. The years prior to that it had been my brother and I. No one ever questioned all the time Mom and Steve spent at nearby hotels for drinks.

My Best Friend Pam

1968, the year I turned 13, my best friend Pam went to Canada with my Mom and I. All of us stayed with Steve in the two room Attic he had rented. Pam and I slept together in Steve's bedroom, Mom slept in the bed in the other room, while Steve slept on the sofa.

That summer, when my friend Pam and I stumbled on Steve and my Mom together in bed, Mom scolded me for having a dirty mind. "I was cold, and Steve was just trying to warm me." Which didn't make sense because it was 80 degrees outside.

My Mom never realized the idea that she and Steve were lovers had never entered the minds of either Pam myself. She didn't realize that I'd never thought of Steve as anything but my molester.

Snapshots from a Broken Camera

Mom was never much of a drinker. When she drank, her personality did a complete 180. If she was around men she'd get this weird look in her eye and become an outrageous flirt.

More Whiskey Please

Steve was a drunk. He drank from the moment he woke up, until he went to bed. His drink of choice was whiskey. He had whiskey in his morning cereal, whiskey in his coffee, whiskey in his tea, whiskey in his water, whiskey on his toast, whiskey with every meal. He even brushed his teeth with whiskey.

Every time Steve opened his bottle of Seagram's, he'd offer some to my Mom. More often than not, she'd refuse. Steve would scowl and complain that she smoked too much. Mom smoked so much that Steve ended up calling her a "chimney". Pam and I would try not to giggle, but the name was too funny NOT to laugh at.

"Your Mom's a chimney." said Pam. "I looked at her and smiled. "I knew there was a reason this place smells so bad." We both broke out in laughter.

My Mom walked in and smiled. "Having a good time girls?" I remember it was almost impossible to keep from laughing.

"Steve wants you both to be comfortable, so he's letting the two of you sleep in HIS room. That way you girls can be together and have a nice vacation. I'll sleep on the nasty old extra bed in the next room and Steve will sleep across the room on the sofa."

Steve lived in an old Victorian home that was falling apart. His upstairs mini apartment was a dive. The mattress we slept on was lumpy and covered with dark brown stains. Our blankets looked like they came from an army navy store. There was NO toilet.

To get to the toilet we had to climb down the fire escape to the floor below us. There was a shower tub there as well. We shared the tub and toilet with an Indian woman named Mindy and her family.

There was no way you could lock the door and no such thing as privacy. When you were taking a bath or shower, more often than not, someone had to use the toilet. Conversely, when you had to use the toilet, someone was taking a bath.

One evening Pam looked at me with sad eyes and said she need to "take a pee". Mom and Steve were out for a "drink", which meant we had the place to ourselves. "Use this cup." I quickly suggested, holding up Steve's special cup.

Sweet Pee

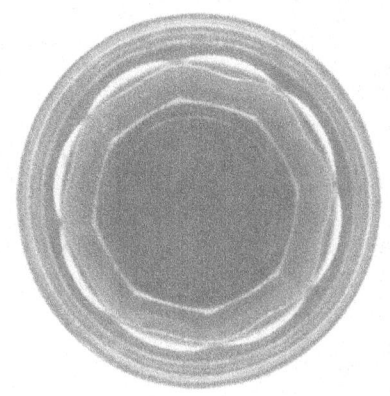

"Nooooo," answered Pam with a shudder. "I could NEVER do that."

"Sure you could." I said, eyeing the cup. "I'll turn my back while you go pee in the other room."

"Now what do we do with this?" asked Pam, holding up the now full glass. "I can't just throw it out the window ... can I?"

I picked up the glass and held it up to the light. "You know this is the same color as Steve's whiskey."

"Noooo Jeanne Noooo," said Pam reading my thoughts "We'll get caught."

I walked over to the kitchen sink and opened the new bottle of Seagram's Steve had placed on the counter this afternoon. I quickly poured a cupful down the drain. "Your Mother will know Jeanne." warned Pam.

"No she won't" came my answer. Then I carefully replaced the missing whiskey with Pam's fresh urine. I returned the cap, wiped down the bottle and handed to Pam. "See what I mean? The bottle looks just fine."

For weeks afterward, Pam and I used any excuse to serve whiskey to Steve and my Mom. At first it was hard not to laugh. Both Steve and my Mom seemed overjoyed at the change in our demeanor. Steve would hug me, (which made my hair stand on end) and hand me twenty dollar bills when he wanted to go out with my Mom. My Mom would smile.

I rewarded Steve by pouring him as much whiskey as he would drink, and by always adding something extra special (spit) in his food.

Snapshots from a Broken Camera

The Summer of 68

In many ways, the Summer Pam and I spent in British Columbia was one of the best I can remember.

Pam and I were free, and whenever we were together nothing bad happened to us. So the high water pants my Mom forced me to wear ... didn't matter as much because no one really cared. The shoes which didn't fit and hurt my feet ... didn't matter as much because I went barefoot whenever I wanted. When I tore a ligament in my foot ... I bore the pain and never made a connection with my wearing too small shoes.

I was free, for the first and sadly the LAST time in my life. I was free.

Pam and I took the bus from New Westminster to Vancouver to Burnaby and back. We walked the streets of "Gas Town" not aware it was a slum. We made friends with the hippies living in a tent outside of Steve's house. We picked fresh raspberries and cherries growing wild in Steve's backyard. We purchased Tarot cards, and 60's posters and cool looking acrylic flowers. We ate freshly battered and fried cod and chips in Stanly Park. Chips with vinegar and salt.

We adopted a pure white kitten we named "Sparky" after our choir director Jack Coleman. We cleaned the cat box out daily. Scooping out poop using one of Steve's special spoons, then tossing it out our bedroom window and onto the roof.

We made fresh popcorn on Sheila's basement stove, despite the fact there was no lid for the pan. Two cups of popcorn seed goes a long way. It snowed popcorn that afternoon, all over Sheila's clean kitchen floor.

Sheila laughed and smiled and melted a pound of butter in another pot, then poured the golden goo over the popcorn on the floor. "Eat well" she said, while laughing and sprinkling salt over the entire oily mess.

Sheila's children, Valery, Bonnie and their older sister sat on the floor with us, giggling and laughing and eating hands full of popcorn. The memory of their laughter will always hold a special place within my heart.

Then Summer ended and Pam and I returned to our homes and the chaos which surrounded BOTH our lives.

For almost four years, Pam had been my friend and sister. During those years we spent most of the time together or on the phone. I felt safe and warm and loved when she was around, because with few exceptions only good things happened when she was there. Little did I know even that would change next year.

The next Summer, the Summer I turned 14, changed both our lives. The car accident changed me, too much I suppose, because suddenly Pam was gone. She had her own heart aches and sorrows to contend with. So for reasons known best to Pam she moved on, and was no longer in my life. (Although she returned a decade later.)

My Grandparents had died and were no longer in my life

My brother had married and was no longer in my life.

Jack Coleman left our church and was no longer in my life.

My Mom still suffered the effects of our car accent and had little time for me.

Dad was in his own world most of the time.

Other than the Siamese cat my Brother had given me the year before, I was completely alone. No one cared.

Snapshots from a Broken Camera

Memorial Day May 2013 ~ Remembering can be Difficult

Even now, over 40 years since the day of my accident, I still bear the scars. (Shattered in the accident) One by one I have lost all but three teeth. I have no feeling in the parts of my left side that suffered soft tissue damage during impact. It almost always hurts when I walk. I developed Dysautonomia as a result of my brain contusion.

I will never look normal. I will never feel normal. I will never go to a school prom ::: never attend a school dance ::: never be a cheer leader ::: never get high school Valentine flowers ::: never be called beautiful ::: never get asked out by a popular boy ::: never get a chance to be a child ::: or have one of my own ::: never get a chance to grow up without pain and sorrow.

I have lived my life striving to attain and maintain grace. An indefinable something which I have used to define my soul ::: the person I am, both inside and out. While I can NEVER forget my past, I have been able ::: to some extent ::: to grow beyond it.

My soul resides someplace between what was and what might have been. A place where hope is both my motivator and my salvation. A place where I can still believe in all that is good and best in mankind. A place where I can be almost anything I choose.

✑June 1973 ~ Santa Ana

Mother Daughter Conversation

Mom to me ...
"I dreamt you were in a car accident during our trip." (who said anything about OUR trip?) Mom was Speaking with a thick Dutch accent. "The force off mine body drove you true da front vin-doe."

My thoughts at the time ...
Hey what's with the exaggerated accent? Yeah right Mom, like you could fit in the back seat of a Honda CVCC, let alone AGREE to sit in the back seat of ANY car.

Mom to me ...
"Zoe... IK (Dutch for "I") Vill ... NOT... GO-INK." In her most dramatic Dutch martyr's voice. Pause for effect and inhale deeply "Zoe you vill NOT die." Spoken almost reverently, in a soft half whisper.

Me to Mom ...
"Glad that's finally settled. Just so you know, a 12 hour drive in Michael's little Honda was never my idea of fun. I really hadn't wanted to go, and had planned on staying home for my birthday."

Mom to Me ...
"Goot goot goot. Dat iss beste for all." In a still thick Dutch accent.

Me to Mom...
"No Mom, now I HAVE to go. Don't you see? If I don't, I'll always be a hostage to your visions and premonitions."

Mom to Me ...
"Mark my words, kiddo, you'll lose your virginity and get pregnant to boot". She hissed, her enhanced Dutch accent suddenly gone.

Me to Mom ...
"Are you kidding! Not that it's any of your business, but I don't believe in sex before marriage. But if anyone could change my mind, I'm sure you could Mom. Besides Mom, if I wanted to get laid that bad I wouldn't drive all the way to San Francisco, I'd do it in the damned backyard."

For the record ...
I went to San Francisco with Michael for my Birthday. There was no car accident, and no one was hurt driving. While Michael tried coaxing me into giving it up, I didn't lose my virginity either. FYI ~ I've never had sex in the backyard. I once had a big glass of "Sex on the Beach" in the backyard, but I don't think that counts.

❧When I Look into Your Eyes

When I look in your eyes
I see the wisdom of the world in your eyes
I see the sadness of a thousand goodbyes
when I look in your eyes

Music by Anthony Newley / Lyrics by Leslie Bricusse

When I looked into my Father's eyes I only saw kindness and NEVER felt fear.

I remember my Dad as caring person, who (unlike my Mom) never laid a hand on me physically, (unlike my Mom) never threatened me, (unlike my Mom) never called me names like stupid, or lazy, or worthless.

When I stop to think about it, the fact that I can have, still have, a deep and abiding love for my Dad is amazing, as my Mom did her best to make me disrespect and despise him. That she nearly succeeded, fills my heart with sorrow and shame.

While my grandparents were alive Dad spent two weeks of every year with them. This simple fact angered my Mom beyond words. Mom saw Dad's love for his parents as proof that he didn't fully love her. She used this proof to fuel her need bad mouth Dad and complain about EVERYTHING she said he did wrong to her friends and family (my brother and I included).

Dad's parents lived in Amsterdam, where both their families had lived for hundreds and hundreds of years. Unfortunately, my family was achingly poor, and Dad's yearly trips caused a great deal of hardship ... or so my mother said. What Mom didn't say, was that Dad's trips were almost free. Dad became a travel agent so he could see his parents.

My Mom told me Dad was selfish. Mom said Dad used his parents as an excuse to leave his family and be with his Dutch girlfriend. Mom said no adult male would leave a beautiful loving wife and family unless he was fucking other women, or so Mom said. But then Mom always had a lot to say about EVERYTHING, much of it untrue.

I'd heard snippets about how my Dad had been affected by the war. How he and his Mom had been forced to hide from the Nazis in the sewers below their home. How Dad had seen Nazi soldiers remove his Grandfather by gunpoint. How all but one of his Jewish Mom's many brothers and sisters died in concentration camps.

Unlike Dad, Mom loved talking about the war. She loved nothing more than spending hours reminiscing about how brave she had been, how beautiful she had looked, and how men of all types had yearned for her nubile and lovely body. She told about the Nazi doctor (an SS officer) she had moved in with when she was 19. How they had worked together to save the lives of countless people during the war.

When I was eleven Mom told me she had been a nurse during the war. A registered Nurse, she had said (which I later learned had been a lie). Mom told me that dozens soldiers would be brought in for medical inspections and told to strip naked. She smiled and said she was so beautiful that each and every man would display their desire by developing huge stiff erections. Like needles on a compass, she had said, they all pointed in her direction. She laughed when she told me how she walked down the hallway and tapped each man's penis with her finger, causing them to deflate.

Mom seemed to take great pleasure in my discomfort. "Please Mama, I don't want to know." I can still see the cruel smile on her face as she laughed at my embarrassment. "Come now Jeanne, you're a big girl." she said slyly "Surely you've heard these types of stories before." When I put my hands over my ears, Mama pulled them away. "Don't be a prude." She laughed in my face "Aren't we best girlfriends? I'm just sharing a secret story with you. That's what girlfriends do. I tell you MY stories and you tell me YOURS."

I was only 11 when Mom began forcing me to listen to her war stories and sex secrets. She'd tell me when she and my Dad had sex and how awful it was. She told me she hated having sex with my Dad. She said Dad was like all men, and only wanted one thing. But he was also a smelly stinky beast. She said the only way she could get my Dad to bathe was to agree to a "date" her code word for sex. Mom told me said she hated sex with my Dad, and endured his unwanted advances for the good of the family.

On nights Dad took a bath, I'd go to bed early and pray I sleep found me quickly. More often than not I'd wake up to the sound of my Mother's laughter as my Dad cried out in pain. "Nell, stop you're hurting me. Stop that!" The sound of my Mother's laughter terrified me.

Once I found Mom masturbating on her bed while reading my Dad's dirty magazines. One moment she was rocking back and forth on bed, the next she removed her hand from her crotch and acted like I hadn't seen anything. She told me she was doing her homework. That she had to read Dad's magazines so she knew what he was going to do to her at night.

She told me she had been (and still was) the most beautiful, most talented, smartest, and most desired woman in the world. Any true communication between the two of us came in the form of competition. Anything special I managed to accomplish withered by comparison with my Mom's talents and achievements.

Mom: Always competing, Always the Best

When I started piano lessons, so did Mom, losing interest only after I began playing better than her. When I drew or painted pictures she would "correct them" for me, erasing any flaws and replacing my work with hers. So I drew and drew and painted every day, until finally I was better than her, and she lost interest. When I learned how to embroider, Mom would tell me I was doing it wrong and remove all the stitches out from my creations.

When I won an award at school, Mom would tell me how she had won something similar when she was younger than I. When I struggled with homework, she told me how stupid I was compared to her. Mom was 36 years older than me. There was no way I could win.

When I tried on make up for the first time, she told me to "Take the crap off your face. You look like SHIT!" She was remorseless, impossible to beat, and loved competition. I hated competition. All I ever wanted was for Mom to love me.

So accepted Mom's benediction that she was beautiful and I was not. I accepted the fact that she and my brother were the smart ones, and gave up any hope of ever being smart or talented at anything of value. (She admitted I was a talented artist, but everyone knows that art doesn't take brains.)

Glamour Shot of my Mom.
One of many taken by my Dad around 1963

Snapshots from a Broken Camera

The Most Beautiful Girl in the World

Mom had always said I would never be as beautiful or desired as she. No one could. She told me endless stories of how every man she had ever met desired her. During the war soldiers had given her gifts of food, chocolates, and silk stockings.

Many men had loved her, the rich ones showered her with lavish gifts, offered her marriage and everlasting love. Years later, men still loved and desired her, they always had and always would. She could ask a man for anything, and they would give it to her.

I remember feeling worthless, ugly and somewhat dirty. I prayed Mom's stories would end. I thanked God I had no sex secrets of my own for her to pry out of me. In my heart of hearts I knew I would NEVER share ANY secrets with my Mom.

Mom told me how Amy (Grandma) broke a carpet beater over her back, because she wanted to date men. When Mom's parents locked the doors to keep her from going out at night, Mom would climb up or down her second story bedroom window. She came and went as she pleased.

Mom Told me she had dated the sons of Fokker and Krupp, visited their homes and factories and flown in their planes. They were rich wonderful men who had treated her like the royalty she was born to be.

Mom: Nazi Collaborator "Moffenmeiden" or Resistance Hero?

Before and after pictures of Dutch Collaborators who had their heads shaven after the war.
National Archives and Records administration, US army photograph, 18 September 1944

I heard snippets of other stories, whispered by several family members, not quite out of earshot. At the end of the war Mom had been taken prisoner and branded a collaborator. She had been a "party girl" "whore", who loved favors and dated several different Nazis during the occupation.

Apparently Mom's father, who really had worked for the underground, came to her aid. He got her released before her hair was cut and she was paraded for all the world to see.

Mom told me she had loved Carl, her rich aristocrat SS doctor / lover, and he had loved her. She moved in with him so they could work together with the underground. She said that her being arrested as a collaborator had been a mistake made by people who didn't know about her work against the Nazis.

Snapshots from a Broken Camera

Dad and WWII

Dad rarely spoke about the war, other than to talk about childhood antics. Peeing in mail slots and getting his "peter" stuck inside a mail slot one memorable afternoon. He spoke with pride about how he started smoking at age 11.

He loved telling me how he and his friends would climb into houses which had been emptied by German soldiers. (They would take whatever valuables the German's had left behind. His elders would hide what they had found, away from the Nazi's, and keep them safe for those who were lucky enough to return home.) He'd laugh at the memories and pat me on the head.

When Time Magazine published pictures of the Holocaust, Dad purchased a copy. That afternoon I found him weeping in the Den. He was alone, the open magazine in his lap. That weekend, he had Grand Mal seizures all night and into the following day.

The next day, I realized the magazine still lay open in the Den. So I decided to sneak in and take a look. What I saw shocked and horrified me beyond words. I saw images of thousands of dead bodies, stripped of their clothing, heaped one upon the other in an incomprehensible tangled mess.

When I asked my Mom what the pictures were about, she gingerly picked up the magazine, closed it, and tossed it under the coffee table. She made a sneer, the same sneer she made when she had found one of Dad's dirty "Sex" magazines. "Don't ask, and don't tell your Dad you saw these. The pictures make him sick."

Indeed, every-time Dad looked at the photos he became ill. Mom tried to throw the magazine out, but Dad flew into a rage, the likes of which I'd never seen or heard before. The sound of him screaming "I can NEVER forget." still echoes in my ears. So the magazine stayed in the den, surrounded by other books on the Holocaust and WWII.

Dad bought countless books on world war two. He watched movies and television shows about the war. The whole family watched war movies together. When Dad saw documentaries or news reports about the Holocaust, he'd get sick. He'd have Grand Mal seizures lasting days, usually on weekends. Mom instructed us not to tell, or Dad would lose his driver's license and possibly his job.

Mom told me Dad started having seizures when she was pregnant with me. The intimation being, his seizures were somehow "my" fault. Which is why it was my responsibility to keep his seizures secret and NEVER tell.

After a seizure Dad would stumble around the house calling for his "Mama". His pants were usually soaked with urine and smeared with shit. The sight of him stumbling like a zombie through the house, stinking of sweat, urine and shit, horrified me.

Once, right after a seizure, Dad walked into my room late at night. He was in a loose pair of urine soaked jockey shorts. Shit covered the back of his now brown underpants and had run down the back of his legs. Drool was dripping down from the corner of his mouth onto my bed. His body moved in stiff awkward movements.

Dad grabbed and shook me in my bed, his body odor was overwhelming and nauseating. Dad didn't recognize me. "Mama, Mama" he cried. I looked into his eyes and I didn't recognize him either. Mom came into my room, grabbed my Dad by the hand and took him to their bathroom. "Mama, Mama", my Dad continued crying out.

I heard my mother talking to my Dad. Her voice was slow and steady, as if she were talking to a small child. "Dick, Dick, Luister wat ik zeg. Je had een aanval, alles is nog steeds ok. Ik zal je schoon maken. Dan moet je terug naar bed gaan." [Dick, Dick, listen to me. You had an attack, everything is O.K. I'll clean you up. Then you need to return to bed].

When I was around 12 I started worrying that my Dad was epileptic and that I would start having seizures as well. My Mom told me not to worry, that I was more Fontijn (her maiden name) than Barkemeijer. "You will NEVER be like your father, so don't worry."

Mom's words were not the answer I expected. Fear shot through my body. I thought, "Dad's NOT my father!" I ran into my room and wept for hours. I loved my father. I couldn't fathom him not being my Dad. If Dad wasn't my Dad, who was? The question lives with me to this day. I look for my face in my Dad's, and see no resemblance. I never have.

But men had always surrounded my Mom. As a child I saw Mom kissing different men in my bedroom. I can only assume they thought I was asleep, or too young to understand anything I had seen. My brother told me he had seen Mom kissing men in his room as well.

For all Mom's accusations of Dad's supposed infidelities, I never once saw him look at another woman, let alone kiss her. In all the years I knew my Dad, I never found a photo of him with someone else, or heard him say he wished he wasn't married to my Mom. He was totally devoted to my Mom, yet she had never been able to see it.

❧ Smoke Signals

I don't know exactly how old I was at the time. I guess around 13, because my brother had moved out. My Grandfather was being cared for in fountain Convalescing Hospital. My Dad was at work, so there was no one in the house except my Mom and I.

I was home on summer vacation and I'd been trying to clean my bedroom (no small task) for the better part of two weeks. Years ago my friend Pam had taught me how to sweep things under my bed or in the closet. Hadn't figured out I wasn't actually cleaning my room, and faking a clean room helped get me out of the house when I really needed to.

Over time, for reasons I don't quite understand I started letting trash pile up on the floor of my bedroom. I can't explain, but I felt safe and calm and protected surrounded by trash.

That summer the trash in my room had started spilling out from under my bed, to my bedroom floor and onto my bathroom and the hallway outside my bedroom door. I also left school books, coats, sweaters and more on the big dining room table in the living room. My Dad also left books and papers and mail on the same table.

In a way, that dining room table never made sense. Our house was small, less than 1000 square feet, and the dining room was only about 15 by 10 feet. Yet my Mom had placed a table large enough to seat twelve, right smack dab in the middle of the room. The table might have been OK had she not also inserted all the extensions for a dinner party. She liked the way table looked so much, that rather than fold it back up, she left it open.

The problem was the room also contained an upright piano, a huge china cabinet and a fireplace at the end of the room. Traversing the room wasn't easy. At best you had to walk around the table, avoiding chairs, drawers, the piano and piano stool, along with any obstacles on the floor. At worst you'd find yourself stuck at the door.

So EVERYONE piled stuff on the table, which made Mom crazy. Both my Mom and Dad were hoarders, this in a time before much had been known about or written about the phenomena.

Mom was a self professed "pack rat" who organized things on selves, in cupboards, closets, boxes, bags and drawers, where she promptly lost them. Dad was an out and out slob, who let everything pile up in his dark room, work room and on top of his office desk.

Every spring, during her yearly manic episode, Mom waged war against mess and clutter. For days on end, she cleaned like a crazy woman, barely eating, not sleeping, and never stopping to rest. When Mom was done, there was a stack of boxes for the goodwill, along with a huge pile of trash set on the front curb. Then Mom collapsed in bed for a week.

The year my Grandfather died Mom's didn't have a manic cleaning episode. I'm not sure why. My Grandfather had been moved to a convalescent hospital and my brother had moved out into his own apartment. Mom spent most of her days visiting with her Dad.

After Opa had his stroke, Mom turned my Brother's room in a hospital room for my Grandfather. She purchased a hospital bed and started caring for Opa Dick's old room. She moved my Brother in to the small apartment my parents had built for Opa in the garage.

When Opa was sent to a convalescent home, the room he'd been staying in was turned over to me. Mom turned my old bedroom, into a storage room. There had always been two closets in my room. I'd only been allowed to use one. Now she had both closets and a room in which to store things.

The room was stacked from floor to ceiling with boxes and other junk. The room was filled with so much stuff you couldn't walk in it, open any of the closet doors, let alone get to, or open, a window. Spider webs and dust were everywhere. When Mom or Dad had something they needed to put away, they simply opened the bedroom door and tossed it in. Suffice it to say the door remained closed most of the time.

When my brother moved out, Dad mostly stopped using his Dark room. The Dark room had degraded into a disorganized tangle of unused photo paper, developing supplies, and trash. The room next door was used store my Dad's tools, and was also piled up with boxes.

Despite all my Mom's complaints and protestations about her constant battles to keep our home clean. She made just about as much mess as everyone else in the house. Mom shopped at the Goodwill for treasures and clothing for me, purchased a lot of "great deals" at various stores, and continued to squirrel away things around the house. The problem was, Mom RARELY threw ANYTHING out. I grew up thinking all of this was normal, and not knowing how to clean things up.

Mom often told me about how clean Dutch people were. She also said how clean her house in Holland had been, and how she never left a mess. She constantly berated me for being such a filthy American sob. I learned later, that there had been both a housekeeper and a maid at my Mom's home who cleaned up messes for everyone.

Snapshots from a Broken Camera

Back then whenever we had visitors, Mom apologized for the house being in such a mess. A mess "I" made, she would say. Shamed and embarrassed, I'd go off to my bedroom and cry.

This week I'd decided I'd change. I'd start by cleaning my room and hopefully make my Mom proud in the process. I grabbed a pile of boxes and paper bags and started cleaning. First I swept up all the trash on my floor. Then I looked through everything, being careful to only throw out trash. The last thing I did was toss my trash in the garbage.

My room was actually starting to look pretty good. The Next day I was surprised and confused to find my Mom standing in my room, along with most of the items I'd thrown away. *"This isn't how we clean Missy."* She said, her arms wrapped tightly across her chest. *"This isn't how we do it at all."*

"But Mama", I said in exasperation. *"Most of that stuff is old and broken."*

"It can be fixed." She answered tersely. *"Anyone knows that. You should know that!"*

"But Mama, what if I don't want that old stuff anymore?"

"Like all your dolls?" said Mom accusingly.

"I didn't throw out ANY of the dolls."

"Liar," shrieked Mom, holding up a broken and battered old doll.

"Geeze Mom, can't you see that doll's broken?!"

"Because YOU didn't take care of her. She died because of YOU Jeanne."

"Your dolls love and need you. They trusted you to take care of them. Is this how you repay their love and trust?" Mom pointed to a box I'd filled with all my dolls. *"By letting them DIE?"*

I sighed deeply. *"Mama collecting dolls was always YOUR idea, NOT mine."*

"Ungrateful child ..."

"Mama, I'm not a little girl anymore."

"Ungrateful bitch! Your grandfathers worked together to build special shelves for your dolls, so you could display them ALL around your bed."

"Mama, a hundred dolls is too many! Besides, the dust is getting to me."

"Dust! DUST! You wouldn't have dust if you bothered to clean your dolls every week."

"I don't want to clean a hundred dolls every week."

"No, you'd rather put them in a box and let them die."

"Look Mama, I've kept 10 dolls I really love. I'll care for them."

Mom ran over to the dolls on my bed, she picked one up and threw it down on the floor and kicked it. *"Why not throw this one away with the others?"*

"Mama," I cried, shocked at her behavior *"all I've been doing is trying to clean my room. Are you telling me if I don't keep ALL my dolls, I can't keep ANY of them."*

"People who traveled the world spent good money to buy you those dolls. Your father's clients, people you've never met, took the time to give them to you. Do you love and care for these special dolls? No! Not YOU, miss I don't want 100 dolls. You should be grateful."

"Mama, I never wanted to collect dolls from around the world. That was your thing."

Mom slapped me in the face. *"Don't EVER talk to me that way ... MISSY!"*

Mom walked over to my bed, picked up the remaining dolls and then tossed them in the box with the other dolls.

"Mom, MOM, what are you doing? Those are mine!" I picked up the one doll I loved best and hugged him to my chest. He was the first doll I'd ever purchased with my own money. I called him Tommy. Mom came over and wrestled him from my arms. I began crying when one of his arms broke off in the process.

"There, now he's dead too. You killed him as well! Now they can ALL go into the trash."

I eventually managed to retrieve my doll Tommy (and fixed his arm) along with the other dolls I intended on keeping. Mom hadn't thrown them into the trash, but had hidden them in my brother's room along with his things. One of her never ending life lessons for me.

That afternoon I gave up cleaning my room. Hopelessly despondent, I wept for hours. I sat on my bed and wrote a six page letter to the pastor of my church. In it I detailed my living conditions, my mother's abuse, and begged him to help me get into a foster family.

Afterwards, feeling better, I tore the letter up into tiny little pieces. I scattered the pieces into the bottom of four paper trash bags, which I then topped off with trash from my room. I placed these bags alongside a bunch of other trash bags already stacked in my bathroom.

Then I lay down on the sofa in the Den so I could watch the sunset from the sliding glass doors. I'd been there about 30 minutes or so when I heard my Mother walk down the steps and into the Den.

She sat down in the chair next to me and began reading out loud. When I realized she was reading my letter, the one I'd torn up and thrown away, my heart literally skipped a beat.

"Life at home is so hard, I don't know if I can take it anymore." Said my Mom in a strange falsetto voice, dripping with sarcasm. "I don't know what I'll do if someone doesn't help me." She sighed deeply, inhaled dramatically and then sniffled loudly.

Something inside me turned. I felt cold inside and out. I got up from the sofa and faced my Mother.

"You think you've won, but you haven't. You think you own me and my thoughts, but you don't." I didn't recognize the voice coming out of my mouth. "You think you control me Mama, but you NEVER will."

For the first time in my life, my Mother was looking at me with fear in her eyes. For the first time she was listening without interrupting my every word.

"You read my letter, so you know that everything I said was true. Never forget Mama, I tore the letter up. I made a choice NOT to send the letter, because I didn't want to hurt you or Dad. You're the one who decided to piece the damned thing together and read it to me. Always remember it was YOU who started this war between us."

"Now it's your turn to be scared Mama, your turn to run and hide. Because from now on, I'm going to go through ALL your trash and read ALL your letters. NOTHING you write or say will EVER be private or safe again! If you write about Dad, I'll give a copy to him. Write about one of your friends and I'll give copies to them."

Later that evening, while my Mom was talking with my Dad, I went through all the trash cans and pulled out dozens of letters my Mom had written and thrown away. Mom was always writing, it was her way of getting things off her mind.

When Dad went to watch TV, I pulled out the letters I'd found, and showed them to my Mom. "What do you want me to do with these Mom?" I asked, my face inches from hers. I waved a crumpled paper at her. "Do you think Dad would be interested in reading this one?"

I took out another crumpled paper, and smoothed it out on the kitchen table. **"Oh look, this one's addressed to Steve. Shall I read it to you? édesapám majom [dear father monkey, my Mother's pet name for Steve] ... Do you need to hear more?"**

I dumped all my Mom's letters onto the kitchen table. **"Here Mom, these are for you. I don't give a damn what you do with them. Just remember, from now on, nothing you write will ever be private again."**

That night I smelled smoke coming from the kitchen. One by one, Mom had placed all her letters on a pie tin and burned them in the kitchen sink. I was standing in the hallway thinking about the day, when my Dad passed me on the way to the bathroom. ***"Your Mother's sending smoke signals." "What do you mean Dad?"*** I asked smiling. ***"Some new metaphysical bullshit she just started."*** he answered with a laugh.

I reached over and gave my Dad a hug. ***"You know I love you Dad."*** My Dad put his hand on my head and mussed my hair. ***"Thanks Shrimpy, I love you to."***

⁊ The Day my Father Died

My dad didn't die in a single day. I have a feeling he'd been dying for a very long time, worn down by events, too many cigarettes, stress, and the passage of time.

About a year before my father died, mom suffered a stroke. One moment she was there, the next there was this angry stranger, unable to speak, residing in her body.

We tried for a year, Dad and I, to juggle our work hours so my mom wouldn't be home alone for any length of time.

I'd start work at 6am, he at 10. I'd come home for an hour at noon to check on her, feed her and give her what medication she needed at the time. I'd be home by 3pm.

We had to disconnect the bathroom wall heater after Mom set fire to our plastic shower curtains. The shower curtains were up against the wall heater (never a good idea) and Mom couldn't tell the difference between the light switch and the heater switch. I remember she tried to wash the molten plastic shower curtains, (thinking that would fix them) metal hooks and all, in the washing machine.

I remember Mom's attempt to cook dinner, filling the pot with so much potatoes and meat there was little room for water. The whole thing turned into a big charred mess. Ever supportive, Dad ate it with a smile. I remember what a nightmare that first year was, and how terrifying it was living with a stranger who looked so much like my mom.

My father was one of those people who always seemed happy about something. He loved talking to people. He'd always manage to know everyone he came in contact with on a first name basis. The check out people at the grocery store, the manager at our Mc Donald's, the pharmacist, all the waitresses at Denny's. His was a gift I doubt I'll ever be able to equal, that ability to show people, in an instant, that they are real… that their life has value… and that this one person cares a great deal about how they are doing.

I watched Dad wither after my mother's stroke. She'd been cruel before, however, her moods always came in waves, like the tides of the sea, and with familiar warning signals. A look in the eye, a tone of voice, a turn of her hand. So we knew ahead of time whenever that hard edge of hers was about to surface.

Dad could tune her out then, at least it looked that way to me. His body was there, while she was ranting, but his eyes had this far away look to them. He'd nod just often enough to let her know he was still attached to the planet. When Mom was done placing blame on one family member or the other for one of our never ending transgressions, Dad returned, body, mind, and soul.

Dad adored my Mom, regardless of how cruelly she treated him. He was like a huge puppy, eager to be loved, willing to endure all for any show of affection, however small that might be. He lived for the days when all went well, when they would sit and drink iced tea for hours and talk about friends, work, the weather and other meaningless things.

That person, the person my father adored, died during my mother's stroke. What was left was hard, cold, bitter, fearful and demanding. She couldn't speak, and blamed us for not understanding her. She couldn't understand us, and railed against the world. Small irony that the first words she remembered were obscenities. Choice tidbits of words, hurled against us daily, making life after her stroke a living hell.

While a year's worth of speech therapy helped my mother regain partial ability to communicate, the woman we knew never returned. I watched my father grow gray blue that year, (inside and out) and withdraw more and more into himself.

I'd been pleading for years with Dad to stop smoking. That year, horrified by the changes in his coloring I begged him again to at least slow down.

"Five packs a day is too much, it's killing you, and the smoke is making us all ill." Dad told me he didn't inhale five packs a day, and that most of the cigarettes burned up in his hands without ever reaching his mouth. One day I looked at him and asked him if he wanted to die. He looked at me with such anger I simply walked away.

Snapshots from a Broken Camera

Three days later I was sitting on the living room sofa watching "Star Trek The Next Generation". My mother came in and told me my father was having chest pains. Without even getting up from the sofa, and going to look at him, I knew he was having a heart attack.

I went to Dad's room pleaded with him to let me call the paramedics, he refused. So I made him a deal, in return for my NOT calling the paramedics he'd let me take him to the hospital where I worked as a respiratory therapist.

When we got to the hospital Dad insisted in walking in on his own. I ran in before him telling the head nurse he was having a heart attack. As I worked there, and everyone knew me, they took me at my word and placed him directly in a cardiac bed.

I went into the nurse's lounge to sit and wait with an R.N. friend of mine. Suddenly, out of the corner of my eye, I saw a shadowy image of my father standing in the hallway beside us. He was talking to his dead father, who I could also see.

I turned to my friend and said "my father's in full cardiac arrest". She looked at me and told me I was just over worried. When I kept insisting he was in full arrest, she told me I needed to calm down and relax.

Suddenly "Code Blue to E.R." came over the intercom. My friend looked at me, and told me to stay there, that she'd check on my dad. She didn't realize I was looking right at him and my grandfather standing in the hallway. I already knew what was going on.

Dad survived his first heart attack. Weeks later, he told a story of standing in the hospital corridor and talking with his father. He said, his father had told him it wasn't yet his time to die, that he had things that needed finishing on earth. I never told him about my having seen the two of them standing together in the hallway outside of the nurse's lounge.

My brother had come to visit our Dad. I told him the story of how I'd driven like a mad woman to get to Dad the hospital before he went into arrest. I was shocked when my brother looked at me and said "Next time drive slower." I didn't know if my brother's statement had been a bad joke, or how to respond.

After his heart attack, my father had insisted on wanting to be home for Christmas, so he could go to my brother's house. A few days earlier I called my dad from work. One of his attending cardiologists happened to be there and I asked my dad if I could speak to him. I expressed my concern that my father hadn't yet had an angiogram. At which point the doctor began screaming at me over the phone, insulting me, and yelling so loudly I feared my father would become ill. I backed down.

When I went to pick up my father early morning on Christmas Eve I could see he was horribly ill. He was weak as a kitten, and his color was off. Again I asked if they could please do an angiogram, again I was rebuffed.

Three days later my father suffered and other heart attack and went into cardiogenic shock. By this time the damage was total and complete. The artery leading to his left ventricle was completely blocked, and had been for too long. Consequently the muscle damage to his heart was now permanent.

That he was even alive, was astonishing. I had made a vow, that I would always stand up for what I believed and/or knew to be true. I would never let anyone intimidate me the way that doctor had again. A hard bitter lesson to be learned, with a horrible cost, the eventual loss of my father.

While my Dad was in the Hospital for the second time, Mom wanted to spend every day there with him. I had to work and I had to take care of my Mom. My period kicked in the day Dad was admitted the first time. The bleeding continued throughout both hospitalizations. I was tired and felt like hell.

One afternoon I came home barely able to move. I'd taken Mom to the hospital every day that week. The day before, when we came home from the hospital there had been dishes to finish, laundry to do, and my Mom had to be fed. I hadn't been able to get to bed until well after midnight. Every day I started work at 6am. I was tired beyond words.

Mom met me at the front door, fully dressed. "I'm ready to go see your father." she said. "Mama, I don't think I can."

"I've been waiting all day to see your Father." Mom, obviously angry, glowered at me. "You're TIRED! Poor baby. SO WHAT!" sarcasm dripping from her voice. "Your Dad is in the hospital waiting to see ME, and YOU'RE too tired to drive me over!"

"Mama, please let me lay down for a couple of minutes, I'm bleeding like a stuck pig and I haven't had a good night of sleep weeks."

I lay down on the den sofa and closed my eyes. 20 minutes later the doorbell rang. Still groggy with sleep, I stumbled over to the front door. The husband of my Mom's best friend was standing outside. He pushed himself inside the house and called my Mother's name.

Snapshots from a Broken Camera

"Nel honey, it's Don. I'm here to pick you up ... are you ready to go?" I suddenly realized my Mom was standing behind me, just out of Don's view. She grabbed me by the shoulders and pulled me roughly out of her way.

Don, a man I'd known all my life, who had never uttered an angry word towards me, was staring at me with pure hatred. "You should be ashamed of yourself." Overwhelmed by Don's unexpected outburst, I didn't know how to reply. "I am Don, believe me I am."

Mom was smiling, a horridly cruel and ugly smile. "You're NOT my daughter." She said with great dramatic flair, and then exited the front door with Don supporting her arm. She was laughing gaily when Don opened his car door and helped her inside.

I near hysterics and crying uncontrollably, I called Don's wife Peggy. "Jeanne, Jeanne, what's wrong?" "Peggy I don't know what I did wrong. I don't know why is Don so mad at me. I've been taking Mom to the hospital every day. I work 12 hours a day, and then I have to feed Mom and do all the housework when we get back. I barely sleep 5 hours a night."

"Your Mom didn't tell us ANYTHING like that. She said your Dad's been in the hospital for weeks and you NEVER take her to see him." "Peggy," I cried, "that's simply not true. All I did was ask her if I could lay down for half an hour. I worked all day, I've gone to bed late every day this week, I'm having a bad period and feel like hell."

"Don't cry honey, Don and I didn't know. Neither of us knew. From what your Mom said it sounded like you weren't working and were too lazy to do anything for your Mom or Dad."

I felt guilty for not taking my Mom to see my Dad. But I was also tired and felt so weak. Mom didn't care. After what she'd been telling her friends, I knew she was going to tell my Dad I didn't care. I stood leaning against the front door crying until I couldn't cry anymore.

The last memories I have of my father are bitter sweet. I'd been running myself ragged during the three months after his last heart attack. After countless midnight runs to E.R. I slept fully clothed, not even bothering to take off my shoes. I was afraid Dad might need to be taken back to the hospital.

I'd change clothing, shower and dress at 4am before work. I'd fix both my parent's medications in the morning, placing them in marked boxes, so they would know what to take and when to take it. I'd fix all the meals, and either cook dinner at night, or bring something home on the way home from work.

In February they discovered Dad had cancer. He was told that both kidneys had fused together, and the cancer had spread to his bladder and possibly his prostrate. The cancer was malignant.

One night, after a particularly bad day with my mother (she'd been calling us both a lot of horrible names), I heard my father utter four words I'd never heard from him before. "I wish I were dead". He'd said, sitting doubled over with his head hanging down almost to his knees. "I can't take much more of this." I sat there, watching him weep, something I'd only seen him do on two other occasions, (both times when my mother had threatened to leave him). "She's not human." he said, tears running down is face.

The day before he died, Dad showed up at my office with lunch he'd picked up for the both of us at Carl's Jr. Dad had gotten into the habit of showing up at work during the last month of his life. I think more to see my brother than me, as I was living with my parents at the time.

However today lunch was for me, because as usual my brother had begged off with Dad. I've been cursed with menstrual problems since my early teens. Dad saw how tired I looked, and asked me if I was having a bad period. I lied and told him it wasn't that bad. I was touched that even with all he facing, he could still see how ill I felt, and say he cared.

That evening I came home from work and told my parents I needed to put my feet up for a bit. I lay down on the living room sofa, and promptly fell asleep. I was woken up three hours later by my dad, holding a McDonald's bag filled with all my favorite foods. "I even got you a hot caramel sundae". He said with a big grin on his face. "Oh and I got you this at the grocery store", he handed me a small chocolate. "I know how tired you looked this afternoon."

I wept and told him how sorry I was for not getting dinner or doing the grocery shopping. He laughed and told me not to worry, that he liked the idea of being able to do something for his two girls (my mom and I). "And besides, we haven't had McDonald's in a long time" (The doctor had told him to stay away from hi-fat foods.)

I ate, and then quickly fell asleep again. Waking only once to see my dad making his nightly rounds to check all the locks and turn off the lights. He waved to me, and called out "good night Shrimpy". I hadn't realized it at the time, but he was saying goodbye.

I woke up 30 minutes later ... in a wild panic. I don't know why, but I felt the need to run to my parent's bedroom.

Snapshots from a Broken Camera

My mother was gone (she in the bathroom with diarrhea) and my dad was in bed having a grand mal seizure. To understand this part of the story, you need to realize that my father had been having grand mal seizures since the year I was conceived. So the sight of him having one wasn't that unusual, or necessarily a cause for alarm. However, something told me tonight was different.

I placed my hand over the artery on Dad's neck and felt for a pulse, it was too fast to count. It felt as if he was in supra-ventricular tachycardia, or ventricular fibrillation. I yelled out to my mother, and told her to call 911.

I listened to my father's chest and heard the distinct sounds of congestive heart failure. His lungs were filled with fluid. Suddenly his heart stopped, and something that looked like thick bright red bubbly tomato soup began pouring from his mouth. Either his left ventricle had completely blown, or he'd just suffered a massive heart attack.

The astonishing thing was, that even without a palpable heartbeat, his hands where clenched and he was still breathing, still struggling to stay alive. So I started CPR. However, by then, so much of blood was coming out of his mouth there was no doubt in my mind as to the extent of the damage to his heart.

I kept remembering how Dad had said that he wanted to die at home, quickly, like his father. I knew that if by some miracle my efforts managed to bring him back, he would be an invalid or worse.

I also knew Dad was facing surgery two days later to remove both kidneys and possibly his bladder. He was told he would spend the rest of his life on dialysis. I knew the cancer was malignant, and as it was kidney cancer. I knew he most likely had metastases throughout his body. So I stopped CPR.

I stopped CPR.

I stopped.

Then I stood back and I let my Father die.

The horror, guilt, shame and confusion of that one instant haunts me to this day. I stopped. I gave up. I let him die. I held onto his hand, and told him how much I loved him, how sorry I was that there was nothing I could do. I felt him squeeze my hand back and I began to cry.

I told him it was OK for him to go, that I'd take care of mom, that everything would be OK. He took one last deep breath, exhaled an impossibly large river of blood, and was silent.

There was a moment, like the opening and closing of a door. During which, I heard my father's voice inside my head repeating over and over "I've got to go, I've got to go, I've got to go, I've got to go," One moment I could feel that energy I'd always associated as the essence of my father, something which had always been there, flicker.

I heard my father's voice one last time, saying, "I'm sorry, I'll be back …". Then the door closed, and the energy was gone, that essence, that something, was no longer there either.

That night my brother's wife Angie came to the house. Over the years she and my father had become close friends. She laughed at his jokes and he at hers.

The coroner had just left. Dad's face and chest were saturated with blood. My Mom was weeping uncontrollably in near hysterics. All my life I'd heard Mom do nothing but criticize and pass judgment on my Dad. So her extreme reaction to his death felt surreal. My world no longer felt familiar or real to me. I was in a fog.

Angie took charge, cleaned and dressed my father. She washed the blood from his face and chest. Changed his blood stained clothing and replaced them with fresh. The last thing we did was put on Dad's socks and his new shoes.

"Under the circumstances I don't think your Mom will mind. I could hold on to them, or give them away. But I hate sending your Dad out in bare feet. " Then Angie chuckled. "Besides, your Dad wasn't a bare feet kind'a guy."

Then we sat together, Angie and I, in silence and waited for Dad to be taken away for cremation. It was well past 3am when they arrived to take away my Dad. I don't remember where Mom had gone off to. Don't remember much else about that horrible night. I do however remember standing outside with Angie while they drove away with my Dad.

I remember thinking Angie's actions, the care she had shown Dad, were the kindest gestures I'd ever seen or experienced.

My Dad died on March 20, 1989 at around midnight, during the Vernal Equinox. What a strange and poetic time to die. To leave a winter of pain, transported into a spring I'm hoping held some measure of peace and joy for him.

Just yesterday morning
they let me know you were gone

I received an email from my Brother yesterday 8/23/13, saying Angie had passed away in her sleep. Angie had been raging war against Multiple Myeloma for the past three years.

Remembering Angie

I met Angie when we were both working at Tustin Community Hospital. She was one of the Med/Surg charge nurses, I was a respiratory therapist. We both worked PM shift.

We hit it off from the get go. Most likely because she had a bizarre sense of humor. A lot of bizarre things go on during PM shit, so her humor was a good fit. Oh the stories I could tell.

My brother was single at the time, and I kept telling Angie she should go out with him. She'd just look at me and say "Naaaah, I don't think so." in that inimitable voice of hers, and wave her hand. "Everyone and their brother has tried to set me up with their brother." She laughed. "I find it's better NOT to date the relatives of coworkers or friends. I find that jobs and friendships last longer this way."

One year when Christmas was coming up, my brother was unusually bummed out. *"Come with me to the hospital Christmas party. You can be my date."*

"You don't need me around, I'll just bring you down." my brother responded.

"Ah gee, if you bring me down I'll just kick your sorry ass the hell out of the party. So I guess you'll have to come up with a better excuse for not coming with me."

Angie and I had said we'd meet at the party, LONG before my brother agreed to be my date. Angie was sort'a kind'a dating someone else at the time.

When we got to the party, Angie grabbed me by the arm. *"Get up and excuse yourself! We have to go to the bathroom."*

"Why didn't you tell me about your brother?" she demanded.

"Are you fucking kidding me?" I asked, looking at her incredulously *"For the past two years I've done nothing BUT talk to you about my brother."*

"Yeah, so what? Girl, you didn't tell me SHIT about your brother, and YOU know it. I mean he's cute. REALLY CUTE! So why didn't you TELL me about your brother?"

I groaned. *"You know you're crazy. Angie, am I done going to the bathroom yet? Can we return to the party now?"*

To make a long story short, Angie took off dancing with my Brother and left me sitting with HER boyfriend, who proceeded to get blind stinking drunk. My Brother took Angie home and basically never slept at his apartment again.

Actually my brother, a man who detests hospitals with a passion unsurpassed in the history of the world, began showing up regularly at my work. He'd nonchalantly amble into my department at break time. *"What'cha here for?"* I'd ask, knowing perfectly well he wanted to see Angie.

"I just dropped by to see if you wanted to have lunch with me."

"Yeah right! Angie's on today. She's in unit three Dick, so go ask HER. Since she's the real reason came here. You are so busted."

Gradually Dick moved in with Angie. Angie had said, *"Dick's at my house so often, he may as well be living here."* Dick and Angie were married on August 16, 1981. They were together for over 32 years.

Snapshots from a Broken Camera

My Sister My Friend

Angie was born in Greece, to a Greek Father and American Mother. On the day I was born, at almost the precise hour, Angie was boarding a plane from Greece to New York, USA ... her new home. You just knew we were slated to meet.

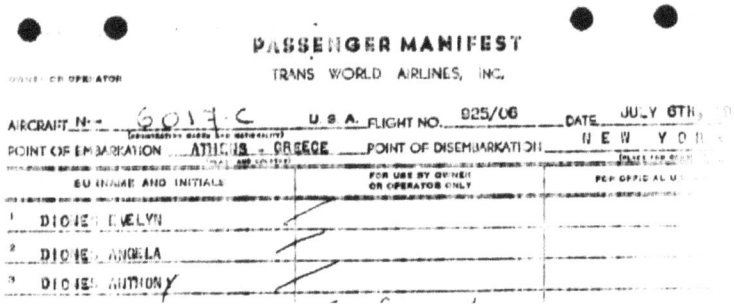

Besides being a Lakota trained Medicine Woman and hospice R.N., Angie played String Bass professionally in several orchestras, most recently the Arapaho Philharmonic in Colorado.

She was also part of the onscreen orchestra in the Dudley Moore movie "Unfaithfully Yours". If you look closely when the orchestra is shown, you'll see Angie playing her Bass.

I miss you Angie

❤

You will always have my heart

I've seen fire and I've seen rain
I've seen sunny days that I thought would never end
I've seen lonely times when I could not find a friend
But I always thought that I'd see you again.

James Vernon Taylor 1970

❧Mama was Dead

February 28 1994

I woke up at five am feeling refreshed and better than I had in years. "Mom", I thought, "I've got to call Mom. She'll never believe it." I'd been bleeding so bad the past three days that I hadn't gone to visit her at the convalescent hospital.

She had been begging to come home ASAP, but she still couldn't walk well enough and I couldn't handle her 300 pound body by myself. After Dad died I cared for Mom by myself. Five years, by myself. I managed to hold on to my job for about three years while caring for her ...

1992 - I passed out while driving home from work. One and a half hour commute home ... one and a half hour commute to work. Low blood sugar. Luckily I'd been able to park the car before the lights went out. 12 hour work days followed by 6 hours spent caring for Mom.

No time to rest, barely time to take care of my needs, it was too much. Eventually I became too ill to go on. I quit my job and cared for Mom full time. She needed me next to her 24 hours a day. She called me so often I ended up sleeping on the floor next to her bed.

My life savings vanished in a year. My health took a nose dive. We lived on Mom's small social security check and my food stamps. I bought the cheapest food I could get. Went to day-old bakeries and discount stores. Still we ran short each month. Three days out of the month I ate nothing so, my Mom and our dogs had food.

When Trader Joe's was selling frozen Lean Cuisine dinners at a 1 dollar a box, I purchased all I could get. Our freezer wasn't that big, so when we ran out I went straight back to Trader Joe's for more. My Mom and I ate Peanut Chicken for months. I hadn't realized that my Mom was getting sick of eating it. I only knew we had good healthy food to eat.

Snapshots from a Broken Camera

My food stamps were gone, and it would be 3 or 4 days before I was able to pick up more stamps, and purchase food for us to eat. It was the end of the month and there was only enough food to feed one person (Mom). When Mom told me she was hungry I did what I had to do. I took the last box of Lean Cuisine and fixed it for her.

When I placed the dish in front of my Mom she looked and me and scowled. "More of this God damned crap?" Then she spit into the dish and threw it on the floor. Mom didn't know I hadn't eaten all day and would have gladly eaten her food. "Junior, Junior" yelled Mama, calling for my greyhound. "Let the dog eat that slurry off the floor."

I looked at the food splattered all over her bedroom floor. "Mama, why in God's earth did you do that?" Mama spat in the direction of the food. "To make a point! Don't EVER feed me that shit again. I'm hungry, now bring me something better, something I can eat!"

I sat down on the floor and started to cry. "Mama, there isn't much of anything left to eat. I have milk, cereal, some noodles, cheese and some cans of mushroom soup."

She pinched her nose with her fingers and grimaced. "I know you have bread and eggs, so fix me an egg sandwich."

"That's all I have left to feed the dogs Mom."

"They're only God damned dogs, they can live with less. I'm your MOTHER!"

After licking all the peanut chicken from Mom's bedroom floor, Junior nuzzled me in the neck. Holding him in my arms, I couldn't contain my tears. Mom looked at me with distain. "What are you crying about? Are you crying about some stupid food? What's your God damned problem?"

"Mama, I've never told you that four days out of the Month, I don't eat. My food stamps and the small amount of money you give me to buy food doesn't begin cover what we eat. I go hungry those days, so you can have food."

"Not eating is stupid! Did I ask you NOT to eat? You think I want you to suffer?!" Mama reached into her purse and pulled out a key. She pointed to a small safe she left next to her bed. She kept her papers, special photos and other odds and ends inside. "Open it open it." I opened the box. "Now give me the white envelope."

Mama opened the envelope and waved a handful of money at me. "Two thousand dollars. Emergency Money. I save this money for years. I hide it in this box."

I was stunned. For months I had gone without, worried about how I could feed everyone. Mama handed me a 20 dollar bill. "Here, here, take this and go quick to McDonalds. Later you take me to the store and I'll buy some food. I have more money in my checking account. Now stop crying."

For years Mom had been telling me she had no money. For years she waited until I spent all my cash to start using hers. "Why didn't you tell me you had money Mama?"

"Jeanne you are stupid girl, not good with money. So I save what I have, or you would spend it all." I didn't know how to respond. When I was still working, before Dad died, before Mom had her stroke, I filled the kitchen with food. I bought my Dad his first color TV and his second. Got my Mom the dishwasher she'd always wanted. I purchased clothing for both of them. I took them both on trips.

I bought my parents anything they would let me, as they refused to accept money from me. Each Wednesday (my day off) I took Mom out to lunch and a movie. I was happy to share. I wanted to be a good daughter.

I cried all the way to McDonalds. It was close to Christmas. I missed my Dad. I missed my brother. I ordered two Children's meals with orange drinks (our regular order) from the car and drove home still crying. I gave Mom her Children's box and drink along with the leftover change. Then I walked outside to eat alone in the backyard.

When Mom slept I played solitaire on the computer and cried.

After Dad died my menstrual periods became longer and heavier. After two years I was bleeding and spotting for months at a time.

I fell and broke my leg ... it was a mess ... I had no health insurance. I went to UCI Medical Center ER and waited to be seen. Four hours later I had to go home and feed my Mom. Swollen and bruised my leg went without treatment. It eventually healed on its own.

I got leftover food from the John Henry Foundation. Fresh cut orange slices, chicken nuggets, corn ... whatever they had that day. It kept us going. A hard five years spent with less of EVERYTHING, and fewer friends.

I had an abscessed tooth ... which I attempted to extract on my own. I got the tooth, but the dead root remained, to be extracted months later. Pain on sorrow on pain.

Snapshots from a Broken Camera

I fainted a lot (I'm prone to low blood sugar) ... at the grocery store, fainted at home ... got to know our local paramedics well. Nightmare life, trying to care for my Mom, our animals, and myself. I've never felt so alone, nor do I ever hope to again.

February 28, 1994 I glanced at the clock on my night table. 5:30am. It was still pitch dark outside. The thought of making one of my daily treks to the convalescent home in the cold dark morning didn't seem very wise. "Mom must still be sleeping. I guess I'll wait. God willing I'll feel this good later on."

I was outside feeding the dogs when the phone rang. I don't remember what was said, or who said it. I only remember suddenly she was gone. Mom died sometime around 5:30 am.

I flew into a wild panic. She was coming to get me. Somehow, someway, she was going to try and take over what little of a life I had. I stood outside shivering, watching my breath turn into great white clouds as it exited my mouth.

Mom had said she'd always be with me, that death would only bring us closer. There was no place to run or hide. I wanted to scream ... to run ... to hide. But where do you hide from the dead?

I'd been suicidal throughout my childhood. I guess no one ever understood why a little kid would want to kill herself. After a decade of yearning for death, at age 16 I downed 100 Valium. A few minutes later I puked them all up. Unfortunately my body had absorbed enough valium put me to sleep. I slept through the weekend. No one noticed.

I had wanted to escape, get as far away as possible, to someplace where even Mom couldn't find me. I believed the only way I could ever do that was to die before her. Now my Mom was dead and a part of me still believed she was coming to get me.

An hour later, when my Mom's spirit hadn't arrived to commandeer my body, my heart rate, my racing mind ... both slowly returned to normal. I was safe, for now anyway, so a part of me went to sleep.

I still hadn't hear from my brother, I'd been trying to reach him for hours. Angie said Dick was already in town. I was shocked, I hadn't known Dick was flying down. Angie said he had arrived in Orange County the day before. Angie didn't know where he was either.

Noon - Dreaming, I entered the convalescent home. Dreaming, I walked into Mom's room and stared into her still open eyes. Her face had a look of surprise. Her long slender hands stretched out as if to touch something. She didn't look dead ... she looked startled.

I reached over to her face and gently closed her eyes, then removed her jewelry. Her hands were warm, unusually so. My ears had started humming and my vision was going fuzzy.

I heard a voice coming from within me, talking to the nurse. I gathered Mom's things and placed them into a thin white plastic bag provided by the nurse. I floated around the spinning room, dreaming, feeling empty and dead, the sound of the ocean roaring in my ears.

7:30pm - I woke up for a moment at the Philip's Hall Theatre. Time for my solo ... I was dressed and ready to walk onto the now blackened stage. The orchestra started playing "Somewhere". I felt my feet propelling me forward, the curtain went up, sound rose up from inside my throat, spilling out over the audience.

> *"There's a place for us,*
> *Somewhere a place for us.*
> *Peace and quiet and open air*
> *Wait for us*
> *Somewhere."*

> **Music by Leonard Bernstein, lyrics by Stephen Sondheim.**
> **From West Side Story**

Two days earlier, during dress rehearsal, Mom had been in the audience looking in. Two days earlier she'd heard me sing. I'd picked her up from the hospital and brought her with me for the day.

The cast and crew seemed to love her and treated her like a VIP. Mom loved the attention. "Jeanne's bringing me home soon." She'd said to them all. I'd seen a ghost image of someone who had looked like Dad, dead five years, watching from the back of the stage. Now they were both gone, and I was alone.

1992 - End games the doctor had called them. "You need to take care of yourself, live your own life, or she'll eat you alive." I felt such overwhelming panic at his words, I was speechless. "I can't", I whispered, "I just can't. God will punish me."

The doctor sighed. "Your Mother wants to control you. She'll use any tool she can to keep you under her thumb, even getting sick and blaming it on you."

I tugged at my top. "Everything's always my fault. I'm a horrible person. She's my mother, she's sick, and I need to do more. Besides, I'm the only one willing to care for her."

Snapshots from a Broken Camera

The doctor pulled my hand way from my top. "You NEED to take care of YOURSELF. You're worn out and sick from the stress of all this. You could end up dying BEFORE your Mom if you don't start taking care of yourself. I don't think she that's what she wants for you."

I felt my insides contract violently followed by sensation of something warm oozing between my legs. "I deserve to die. Besides, I feel so tired and sick I'd rather be dead." I felt the room tilt on its end, and I let my soul glide silently onto the ground.

After my session ended I went to the bathroom. I wiped myself. The tissue was covered with blood and clots. I'd been bleeding three months straight. This was the worst it had been in months. I felt weak sick and dizzy.

1966, the year I turned 11. - "Mama?" She was slumped over the kitchen table, nursing one of her ever present glasses of hot tea. "Mama?" I touched her back.

"What in the hell do you want?" Mama hissed at me, her eyes full of rage. "Can't you see I want to be alone."

The sound of her voice echoed in my brain. I want to be alone ... I want to be alone ... I want to be alone ... I want to be alone ... I want to be alone ... I want to be alone ... I want to be alone ... I want to be alone ...

"Mama," I said, longing to love and be loved. "I think you need a hug. I think we both need hugs. It's been such a long time since you've hugged me. Can I give you a hug Mama?"

My mother shot up from her seat. "You stupid selfish bitch!" She raged, towering above me. "You thoughtless selfish little bitch." My ears started to hum ... I felt my face blush red with shame. "I'm sorry Mama, I thought giving you a hug ..." Mom slammed her fist down hard on the kitchen table, rattling her tea cup and shutting me up instantly.

She placed her right hand over her heart and began talking in a coarse whisper. "You're killing me." Tears started flowing down my face. "I'm sorry Mama, it's been so long. I love you and thought a hug might make us both feel better."

Her face now ashen and her lips grey, my Mother began to scream. "Shut up you stupid little bitch! You're killing me." She clutched her chest even more tightly. "You stabbed me with a knife."

I looked at the knife on the kitchen table. It was laying next to a freshly peeled orange. The thought that I'd just stabbed my mother terrified me.

I imagined I saw blood. I began crying and howling like a wounded animal. I couldn't remember picking up the knife or using it, didn't remember hurting Mom, but obviously I had. She said I had. She was dying, and I had killed her.

My mother was following me around the kitchen, screaming on the top of her lungs. "SHUT UP, SHUT UP, you're KILLING me you stupid little BITCH! I'll die if you don't SHUT UP!"

The sound of her screams echoing in my ears, I ran wildly back and forth inside our tiny kitchen. "SHUT UP and stop crying!" Horrified and blind with fear, I was no longer human. "I'll drop dead right here if you don't SHUT UP!"

She screamed and I slammed into the stove. She screamed again and I ran up against the fridge and kitchen cabinets. I saw her enraged face coming towards me and I crashed into the back kitchen door. "You're KILLING me!" Trying to get away I ran repeatedly into the back door until, waiting for it to open on its own.

Each time Mom screamed, I'd ram into the kitchen door. I was trying to run outside but no longer knew how to open the back door. Finally, blessedly, I lost my footing on the linoleum and I slid violently onto the floor.

I lay on twitching the ground, crying uncontrollably. I wanted desperately to stop crying, but I was filled with such intense fear, pain and sorrow, that I couldn't. "I'm warning you!" Mom kept screaming." I gripped my long hair with my hands and pulled, yanking out large chunks. I felt no pain. "I'll die right here."

Suddenly Mama was towering over me, a large blue metal turkey oven - full of water - dangling over my head. "SHUT UP or I'll die." She threw the pan on top of me. Missing my head by inches.

My legs ached from the weight of the pan. Sore, wet, and impossibly cold, I looked up at my mother. A hard brittle smile was blossoming across my Mom's face. The pupils of her eyes were big and black, blacker thank I'd ever seen. She had on her 5 inch stiletto shoes. She was tapping them on the linoleum. She looked like she was getting ready to kick me.

The hatred in her face chilled me to the bone. The realization that she was close to killing me startled me into silence. I was finally able to stop crying.

"LOOK what YOU made me do!" she screamed "You stupid selfish little bitch." And so the litany began. She raged at me for hours that afternoon, as I lay bruised and wet and shivering on the floor.

Snapshots from a Broken Camera

Then ... as suddenly as it began it ended. "Your Dad will be home soon. I need to fix dinner. But by then I was already mostly gone. Too far gone to realize my friend Pam had been hiding in the living room all afternoon, quietly watching the whole thing. I vanished. I climbed into a place that was safe warm and quiet. It was a long time before I returned.

March 1 1994 - Midnight

I walked into the kitchen and got a glass of milk. I looked at the back door, the same door I'd fallen against almost 30 years earlier. Overwhelmed with grief, sorrow and guilt, I slid down onto the floor, the milk tumbling out of my hands. I lay my head against the door and cried. Mama was dead, and a part of me believed it was my fault.

I was flooded with the memories of another night a thousand years ago. I wondered if these memories were real or were part of a bad dream. The next day I called my friend Pam and told her what I had remembered. "Do you think I'm crazy? Could this have happened?"

"I was there Jeanne." My ears starting to hum. "You were there?" I half whispered. "Yes Jeanne, I saw the whole thing. You didn't dream it. It happened just like you described."

Life after Mom

I can barely remember the days following my Mom's death. I was flooded with memories and other sensations. My roommate had moved out, my house was a mess, and other than my dogs I was completely alone.

I remember going through the house and throwing things out. Sometimes it felt as if Mom loved things more than people. I grabbed dozens of things she had loved ... old vases, plates and other old junk ... smashing everything to bits in the trash can. I dumped out drawers and closets and selves full of glassware, trash, old clothing and rat infested sheets.

When I was too tired to go on, I lay down on the floor with my dogs and cried. My Mom's room was filled with mountains of trash bags she had filled with all her treasures. Stacks and stacks of old newspapers, piled upon plastic bags and trash and junk.

She'd been asking for her clothing for weeks. She had said I had lost her things. I found a mountain of her things, her missing things, piled up in bags around her room. I took everything and dumped it on the front yard. A six foot high pile of clothing and shoes covered the entire yard. It vanished during the night. The next day neighbors were at my door asking if I had more. I continued dumping things for days.

My life Behind the Glass Box

After school I'd watch the 4 O'clock movie, and dream the actors in them were my real family. I was raised by Shirley MacLaine, Gene Kelly, Joanne Woodward and, Fred Astaire. Audrey Hepburn was my older sister, Grace Kelly the Mother I'd always dreamt of.

I dreamt I was Mimi Gibson (the daughter of Cary Grant) in the movie "Houseboat", or Linda Bruhl (Jackie Gleason's Daughter) in the movie "Papa's Delicate Condition".

I'd watch Dark Shadows and dream Barnabas was my friend and my protector.

In 1969, when Star Trek went into reruns I made the starship Enterprise my home. When I watched the show, I felt safe and cared for. For years I pretended the starship Enterprise was my home and its crew were my friends. After the car accident, I dreamed Dr McCoy healed me. I was free to travel the universe. I was free to be anyone I imagined.

As a kid I was sick a LOT. When I was home sick I'd watch reruns of "Father Knows Best", "Leave it to Beaver" and "Mayberry". Betty was my loving older sister, Kathy my younger sister, Bud my Brother. I'd imagine I was living with them, and there was no pain and no sadness and I wasn't alone. Beaver, Wally and Opie were my friends. Mom and Pop loved me, took care of me, and comforted me when I was ill.

I had a small tape recorder, which I used to record the audio portions of my favorite shows. Shows I loved to hear. At night, when I was sad or scared or overwhelmed by life ... I would lay in bed listening to the voices of people I loved, seeing each scene again in my head. Eventually falling asleep feeling safe and warm and loved.

Even now, some 40 odd years later, when I can't sleep or feel sad, scared or overwhelmed by life ... I turn on the television and listen to the voices of people who sound like friends. Friends I don't have, but would love to know. Eventually falling asleep feeling not quite as scared or alone.

❧Living with Panic

Written in 2000 prior to Gall bladder surgery (12/03/2001)

and my diagnosis of Dysautonomia and Fibromyalgia (2008). I'd been taking 2mg of Xanax per day for almost two decades, (equivalent to 40mg of Valium).

A few months before writing this, my then new Kaiser primary physician called me an addict. She also stated 2mg was a small amount and said I could stop Xanax cold turkey. Which I did. Four days later I hadn't slept in days. I ended up in E.R. dehydrated, manic, nearly psychotic, with my electrolytes, blood sugar and vital signs completely out of whack.

The E.R. doctor immediately reinstated Xanax, and told me going cold turkey could have triggered seizures and possibly killed me. The doctor also told me Xanax is almost impossible to get off without help, and should never be discontinued abruptly.

In July of 2003 I began what was to have been a two year slow taper off Xanax. One year later I was completely drug free. I did so on my own, without any medical support, and remained completely drug free for 7 years afterward.

In 2010, after the deaths of my husband's father and brother, I was diagnosed with PTSD and placed on Lorazepam. I look forward to the day I'm again drug free.

Panic

I don't know how long I've actually had panic disorder. I know I've suffered from Panic symptoms for almost as far back as I can remember. My particular situation is complicated by the fact that I also have a number of other medical and psychological conditions which can trigger symptoms mimicking panic disorder. Also suffer from different food and medication allergies. Unfortunately an allergic reaction to any these substances can also trigger full blow panic attacks.

Fear is a terrible thing to live with

As a child I remember going to bed and wondering if I'd wake up in the morning. I didn't know what was making me sick. I only knew I felt sick most of the time. Sometimes I felt as if I were dying.

I suffered from chronic diarrhea throughout my childhood. I remember my family going to IHOP eat. Unfortunately EVERY time I ate pancakes, I always ended up running to the bathroom to vomit. I'd shake for an hour or so afterward. The same thing often happened after I ate donuts (which my Dad bought every weekend).

When I ate the regular sugar infested breakfast cereals popular with children I'd be so hyper I could hardly concentrate in class. After meals I almost always suffered an upset stomach, sometimes I'd end up puking my guts out, I almost always had some sort of diarrhea. In any event, the end result was a child who felt sickness, pain, or terror a good portion of the time.

Mom always blamed all my physical symptoms on me. I was told EVERYTHING was "all in my head". That "I" was making myself sick, I was a hysterical child. I thought too much, prayed too little, ate too much or too little, or too fast, and was an impossible child.

I heard my mother say "I don't love you right now" so many times I began to believe I was unlovable. She'd scream those words at me while also screaming I was killing her (translation: she couldn't handle the sound of me crying) ::: something I'd done ::: my tears ::: hysteria ::: demands ::: anything I'd done she found fault with. At which point she'd slam the front door in my face and dramatically stomp off.

Snapshots from a Broken Camera

I'd lay weeping, lord knows how long, trying to figure out what I'd done to make my mother hate me. I learned to hate myself, and the sound of my mother's car starting up in the driveway. My mantra as a 4 year old was "people say and do things … then they go away". I'd rock and whisper that statement over and over again, while willing the tears to end. Sometimes, when that personality surfaces, I hear those same words coming from my 45 year old mouth. In my mind I visualize embracing and comforting the fearful child I once was, the one living inside me now.

NOTE:

In 1997 I discovered that I suffer from Celiac Disease. This basically means I can't eat anything containing wheat or gluten (that's a lot of stuff). One of the symptoms of Celiac Disease is hypoglycemia (low blood sugar), and lactose intolerance (can't eat or drink dairy products), two problems I was diagnosed with as an adult.

Ironically both of these are symptoms of untreated Celiac Disease. In most cases, these symptoms stop after following a gluten free diet (the stomach lining actually heals). The symptoms of a low blood sugar episode (nausea, blurry vision, rapid heartbeat, mental confusion, the shakes) can mimic and/or trigger a full-blown panic attack.

During my childhood I used to wake up in the middle of the night with the shakes, nausea, and a racing heartbeat. The longer I waited to tell my mother, the worse these symptoms would get. So naturally I'd wake my mom up. (What else can a four year old do?)

My mom, god bless her, would quickly get up from bed, pull out her bible, and we'd go to the kitchen where she'd make hot tea for the both of us. After she gave me a cup of hot tea, laced with a liberal amount of sugar, she'd open her bible at random, and start reading. If that didn't work fast enough, she'd give me one of her Valium.

Twenty minutes or so later my shakes would stop and I'd go back to bed. While I believe in God, and the power of faith, it was the sugar in the tea or the Valium, not my mother's bible reading which eased my low blood sugar symptoms .

When I entered high school and started eating food from the school cafeteria, my panic attacks began to accelerate. Immediately after eating lunch my heart rate would skyrocket, and more or less stay at around 120-140 beats per minute for at least an hour. Which scared me to death.

I remember one memorable occasion when I phoned my poor father at work (My Mom wasn't answering the phone). I was in complete hysterics, and told him I couldn't feel my heart beat. God love him he came right away to my school, and talked my mother into taking me to the emergency room.

Unfortunately my mom had already determined that all my symptoms were in my head, and told the doctor as much. The worst part was laying on the emergency room bed listening to my mom speak about me as if I weren't there. (No wonder I always felt invisible around her) I didn't know the 11 year old she was describing to the doctor.

Mom conveniently forgot to mention frequently blue lips, fingers and toes, chronic diarrhea, vomiting and stomach upset, or my history of chronic anemia.

After listening to Mom ,no doctor ever examined me and no tests were ever ordered. I was diagnosed a "hysteric" and treated as one. This despite my having an extremely rapid and irregular pulse. I was given Mylanta for my stomach upset, my first tranquilizer injection, and sent home higher than a kite.

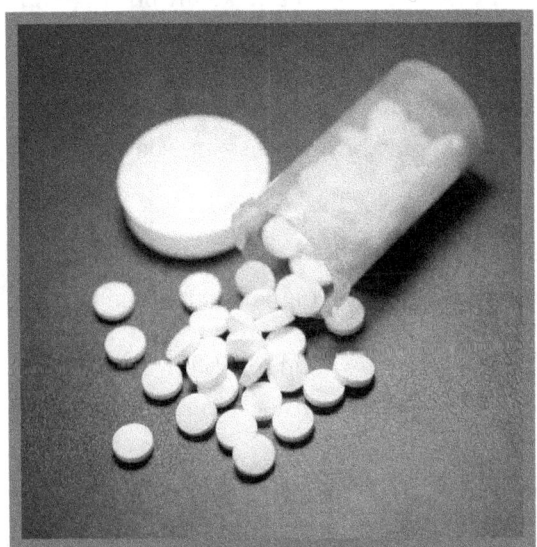

Not long afterward my mother went to an orthopedic doctor friend she knew, and had me placed on Valium. However, I was also taken to the emergency room for treatment whenever my feelings of panic progressed to the point of hysteria, (usually just prior to the start of my menstrual period). So the tranquilizer injections continued for years, and I got to know the E.R. doctors really well.

At the age 16 I was taking anywhere from 25mg – 50mg of Valium per day. That's between 5 and 10 pills a day!!!

(I was only supposed to be taking 5mg a day.) By this time my mother had managed to procure prescriptions for both my father and herself, which she and my Dad rarely took. The bottles Mom got from her physician friend contained 500 - 1000 pills.

Needless to say, between the injections and pills, I was completely addicted to these meds. I remember I'd start getting the shakes 20 minutes or so before it was time to take more meds. I hated the fact I had no choice but to take these meds, and felt as if my life were completely out of control.

Snapshots from a Broken Camera

We now know how addictive benzodiazepines are, the side effects they cause, and the damage the do the brain. I spent most of my childhood being force medicated on one benzodiazepine or another. I also spent an additional 20 of my adult life on Xanax. So I'll never know what it's like to have a normal brain. The saddest part is that I really wasn't given a choice ... so by the time I was old enough to say no ... I didn't know I could.

My mom was a paranoid schizophrenic, malignant narcissist, suffered from Borderline Personality Disorder along with Bipolar Disease, and may also have suffered from Munchhausen by Proxy.

Some days she was OK, other days she'd torture me physically and/or emotionally. She seemed to enjoy watching my pain or fear.

My mom claimed to have been an RN in Europe, (which I later discovered was untrue), read an inordinate amount of medical books, and had a lot of "doctor" friends. I spent most of my early childhood being ill, as my mom thought it was a good idea to take my brother and I over to play any kid suffering from any communicable childhood disease.

She thought we might as well get through all the diseases quickly, together. Less work for her I guess. The only difficulty I have with that is the fact my brother is seven years old and seems to handled being sick a bit better than I.

My dad had hypoglycemia, and suffered from what I was told was a stress related seizure disorder. Judging from my own Tourettes symptoms I'm pretty sure he had it as well.

I was sexually abused for throughout my childhood by a family friend (my Mom's Lover), and emotionally abused by my mom for as long as I could remember. You can more or less imagine how chaotic my childhood was.

I've spent my entire life (I'm 45) doing whatever I could to grow beyond my disabilities. I underwent years of therapy, changed my diet when I discovered I had Celiac Disease, and listened to my doctors. I went to school to become a respiratory therapist. I worked for over 15 years before crashing and burning (translation: psychiatric hospitalization) when my uncle died at home in 1984 after a massive heart attack at age 44. (I'd been doing CPR on him at the time and felt responsible for not being able to revive him.)

I tried to get things together but I wasn't able to return to work in the medical field. I studied computer programming and eventually returned to work the next year for a major computer firm. A job I held until 1991, about a year after the death of my dad (boy am I tired of doing CPR on family members). At which point I crashed and burned yet again ... (isn't guilt a wonderful thing)

When the strain of caring for my mom (she'd had a stroke a year prior to my dad's death), and holding a full time job became too much, I became too physically ill to continue work. I was passing out so often I knew almost all the paramedics in my area on a first name basis.

I was forced to quit my job when I passed out one day during the hour and a half drive home. Luckily I was able to stop and pull over the car before the lights went out. I was eventually diagnosed with hypoglycemia and something the doctor called post adrenal syndrome, (don't bother looking it up, I couldn't find it either). The Dr said my body had been under so much stress for so many years that it had screwed up my endocrine and immune systems.

I enrolled my Mom in college where she was able to receive treatment for the damage done by her stroke. I also enrolled in college at that same time, so I could be on campus with her and earned some 50 units towards a Journalism degree.

We were horribly poor, (I used up every penny I had in savings, and I ended up on food stamps). I took care of my Mom, without help from friends or family, until her death, five years later in 1994.

The act of simply living was heartbreaking and indescribably difficult. 4 days out of the month, there wasn't enough food me to eat. It was the only way I could manage to feed my Mom. Mom had Medicare and got regular treatment. For years I had no money for insurance or medical treatment. So broken bones (I fell and fractured my Tibia - I still have the scar) and infected teeth (I pulled it out myself) went untreated.

I returned to work with my previous employer two weeks after my mom died in 1994. Sadly, by that time, I was too physically ill to maintain my previous level of work. I crashed and burned –yet again– a year later, on the anniversary date of my mother's death.

One memorable afternoon in 1994 I developed a hypertensive crisis and nearly stroked. I was given an ultimatum, either go on blood pressure medications (which made me horribly ill) or go on Prozac.

After years of trying countless anxiety and depression meds, I wasn't all that thrilled with the idea of trying anything new. To a one, every medication I'd been placed on before had made me horribly ill. So it was with great trepidation I agreed to go on Prozac. Amazingly it turned my life around, and I started getting better.

I continued with my therapy, and learned how to design web sites. I started doing volunteer work for a non-profit organization in my area.

Unfortunately in 1999 (after two years of being on a Gluten free diet) I developed a number of side effects to the Prozac and needed to get off these meds. I did fine, and for six months I felt better than I have in my entire life. Previously when I had stopped taking Prozac, the anxiety and depression returned within weeks. I thought I was finally cured of my depression and anxiety. The general assumption being, that a great portion of my anxiety symptoms were actually allergic reactions to food and/or medication.

Three weeks ago I had another hypertensive crisis, and with it the panic attack to end all panic attacks. As the hypertension occurred within minutes of eating something which most likely contained soy (which causes my blood pressure to shoot through the roof), and my blood pressure has since returned to its regular low state, I'm sure the hypertension wasn't panic related.

I've been doing a great deal of research into the causes and treatments of anxiety and/or panic disorder. The latest news points to bio-physiological changes that occur after chronic exposure to CRF, a hormone called "corticotropin-releasing factor" produced by the hypothalamus. CRF causes the pituitary gland to produce excess "adrenocorticotropic hormone" (ACTH), which then makes the adrenal gland release cortisol. These hormones (CRF, Cortisol, and ACTH) are the biological measurements of stress.

The research I've read hypothesizes, that in certain individuals (e.g. those having been exposed to chronic stress and/or abuse) the signal to release CRF triggers way too easily. The unfortunate side effect being an increase in the level of stress hormones in their system, which cause the symptoms associated with depression and anxiety.

The clinical studies I've read seem to indicate that people whose bodies create too much CRF end up suffering from a great many diseases, like major depression, anxiety-related illness, and a number of inflammatory disorders.

In order to stop the cycle of anxiety, which would appear to start within the hypothalamo-pituitary-adrenal axis, they / us / we need a corticotropin releasing factor (CRF) antagonist. Or rather, some sort of medication which blocks the initial stress trigger. Initial studies suggest that CRF antagonists may provide a novel agent for treatment of depression, anxiety and other CRF related illnesses. Unfortunately these types of medications are about five years from being on the market.

So here I am, scared witless, waiting for the you-know-what to hit the fan. I'm suffering from almost constant irrational fear, and nothing I seem to do helps. Some mornings I'm barely able to move, as I'm so paralyzed by the feelings.

My hands get cold, I shake, my heart pounds, and I'm unable to think rationally. Basically I feel as if I'm going mad or dying and I have absolutely no control to stop it. When I take the Xanax regularly I do pretty well. However, it tends to make me feel a little fuzzy headed at times, and mostly I really hate taking these kinds of meds. The memories of my childhood, combined with the stigma attached to taking them is a little much. So I keep trying to taper off, so far without any success.

Then there's this big black cloud hanging over my head, as I'm terrified of if-or-when another attack will begin. I don't want to take Beta blockers, as they only reduce adrenaline levels in the blood, and do nothing to stop the cycle from starting over and/or continuing. Oh, and I've absolutely no desire to experience the types of side effects I went through when I took them before.

I've read that benzodiazepine based medications actually stop the CRF cycle from beginning, more or less stopping the process in its tracks. Apparently there's some sort of benzodiazepine receptor in the brain, which allows this to happen. I guess I need to know it's OK for me to take these meds and not feel guilty, stupid, or like I'm being a pain in the butt to my medical doctor. Who I'm sure thinks I'm nuts for having these ideas.

I start college again in two days, something I've been working towards for months. I keep yearning to earn a PHD in psychology so I can help others like myself. Feeling the way I have these past three weeks, I don't know if I can carry it off.

I'm learning to live with the food and medication allergies, and the physical reality of having a misshapen spine and legs. I want is to find a way to function normally enough to get through life without constantly feeling sick or fearful. Most of all I want to get off of disability and start living a productive and helpful life.

I wish there were some sort of consensus as to the definition and treatment of panic disorder. This whole "Nike" – JUST DO IT– mentality I keep coming up against is making me nuts. I defy any sane individual to remain calm while experiencing explosive diarrhea, extreme tachycardia, and or hypertension. I further defy these same individuals to JUST get up and DO IT, when they feel as if they're dying.

Snapshots from a Broken Camera

God help me. God help us all. Please give me the strength to hold it together long enough to get through another day, please let tomorrow be better. Please help me overcome the fear so I can get up and walk and swim so I don't end up in a wheel chair again, please help me to eat without fear, finish school, and to hopefully make a difference, for myself … and others like me.

Thanks for reading this and letting me vent. Today was a really REALL bad day.

✎6am and All is Well

For as long as I can remember, I've always woken up around 6am. For me 6am has always been sacred. Forgotten were the tirades, accusations, nightmares, pain and terror. I'd survived yet another day and night. I'd made it to twilight, my in-between world, where I was safe and could be anyone or anything I imagined.

Even as a three year old, I'd be up silently padding from room to room to room … a ghost in miniature … checking on family members. I'd pause before each door and send out mental hugs … then whisper … "I love you" and blow a kiss. I felt safe and warm and loved.

At 6am I could love Mama without fear, she looked peaceful and loving and good. Papa looked peaceful and loving and good. Every morning I prayed this would be the morning they woke up happy. That somehow the anger and rage had leaked out of them, through the hardwood floor, magically vanishing underneath the house.

Sometimes I'd sneak out to the backyard and watch the early morning sky shed its heavy evening mantle, and listen to the birds starting their morning rounds. If I was lucky I caught a glimpse of twilight, a world between worlds, were everything was new and fresh and clean … and full of possibilities. I'd take a deep breath, hold it, and pray today would be better.

In 1959, a few weeks after I turned 4 Mom woke up happy and excited. She dressed me up and told me we were going someplace special. She said I was going to start Kindergarten. I knew my brother went to school, but didn't really know what was involved. Mom had said "Kindergarten was like school, only better".

Prior to Kindergarten, I'd never spent much time around kids my own age. Mom basically took me with her every place she went. She'd attach a harness to my waist with a long leash attached to it. When I got too far she'd tug hard to get me back. More often than not I ended up on the ground.

When I arrived at school, I couldn't help noticing that everyone was bigger and older than I was. Trust me, two years is a huge difference to a four year old. The thing is, when Mom was angry at me she'd tell me she was going to send me away. I'd never been away from my family or my Mom, so I assumed I was never going home again.

Once I began crying I couldn't stop. A black haired woman was reaching for my hand. "Mrs. Barkemeijer your daughter only turned four a month ago. Perhaps she's starting too early.

Snapshots from a Broken Camera

You could wait until next year when your daughter's the same age as the other Children." Mom scowled at the teacher, "Jeanne turns 5 during this school year so legally I can start her now. I'm NOT taking her back home."

My Mom pushed me toward the stranger and turned to leave. "I screamed for her to come back." My Mom never turned around. A blond little girl called me a baby and then punched me in my gut. "Bay bee … bay bee … bay bee … bay bee … bay bee … " came the taunts from the other children. Little did I know that these taunts were but a small taste of things to come. Suffice it to say, Grade school sucked.

I loved our backyard. We basically had a cottage there, a sort'a kind'a mother-in-law house my Dad turned into a dark room. Behind the cottage was a perfect 20 x 6 space which I made my own. Behind the cottage was a chain link fence, almost completely overgrown with ivy. I could look out to the word beyond, but the world couldn't see me.

To get behind the cottage I had to push thru an untrimmed outgrowth of trees guarding the entrance. The ground was covered with the remnants of a million forgotten days, fragments of ancient newspapers and leaves and grass and fern.

I was safe in the backyard, behind the trees, the cottage or under the leaves. I was invisible and no one could hurt me.

There was a ditch behind the house, a dirt access road beyond the ditch, and a regular paved road beyond the dirt road. The street was separated from the dirt road by another chain link fence. I loved that magical ditch. It ran down Raitt Street skirting Luken's Dairy and all the cows, across Edinger, past our home, past McFadden and beyond.

One early spring my brother scaled the tall chain link fence with a bucket. When returned from the ditch, his bucket was filled with a swirling mass of black green tadpoles. We spent weeks watching the tadpoles morph from fish to impossibly small perfect tiny frogs.

One day, on a still cool summer morning, we awoke to a house full of miniature frogs. My brother and I went from room to room, scooping up wiggly handfuls of bouncing green energy. We spent most of the morning transferring frogs to an aquarium my brother had prepared for them.

When the city of Santa Ana started using guppies to control mosquitoes in the ditch, my brother again scaled the chain link fence to catch some. The aquarium had been changed from a frog terrarium back into an aquatic home for fish.

I thought those guppies were the most beautiful things I had ever seen. I spent the entire summer watching them grow into colorful mama and papa fish. I cried and cried when one of the pregnant mama fish ate her babies as they were born.

I don't know why, but I can't remember ever being comforted by my Mom when I cried. I guess Mom saw crying as a God given opportunity to give another of her never ending and long winded lessons on life.

I learned at an early age to hide my emotions from my Mom, and to never ever cry in front of her. My crying bothered Mom. More often than not Mom used my tears as an excuse to attack.

I learned to cry alone. I cried behind closed doors, underneath my bed, or in the closet. I cried in the bathtub, under the clothes line, or at the back of our cottage. The cottage was where I felt safest. I'd lean into the cottage back wall ::: tears running down my face; my body hugging the stucco until my face and arms were pockmarked from the wall's harsh touch. Shielded by trees and ivy and stucco walls I simply ceased to be.

Sometimes my only connection with the world was the sound of my Dad's TV blaring in the distance. When the stucco wall became too cold and hard I would simply lie down. The universe spun, stars rose and set, time paused and started and paused again, while I lay buried beneath a blanket of dead leaves, trash and insects.

In 1970, a month after the car accident, Mom started bleeding from her rectum. The doctor was called and I was told to get out of the way. Rather than go down the hall to my room, I stood in the backyard beside the cottage. The sunset sky was awash in vivid tropical colors.

My Dad, overwhelmed by the sight of blood and the sound of my Mom crying out in pain, came and stood next to me. I stood mute, and tried focusing on the sunset. My Dad was seeking solace and comfort from me, only I had none to give.

In my mind, I believed my Dad's was responsible for the accident. If not for his lunch, and the tickets he purchased things could have been different. No accident, no broken bones, no torn muscles or bruises. When I came home from the hospital my Dad offered me no comfort, no solace and no care. When I screamed in terror the first time in a car after the accident, Dad screamed at me to shut up. When I cried he called me names and berated me for acting like a child. The fact that I was a child was beside the point.

Dad placed his wet tear stained face against mine and told me he was scared, told me he didn't know what to do, told me he felt alone.

Snapshots from a Broken Camera

I'd never seen my father cry before, this man who weeks before had screamed at me to stop crying. The stench of his body odor (tobacco and sweat) sickened me. When my Dad hugged me ::: for the first time in over a decade ::: I felt nothing but disgust.

Dad was squeezing my still bruised and battered body so hard it hurt. I longed to pull away ... to run ... but his hold was too strong. So I stood frozen like a statue, in pain, unwilling and unable to move. My Father, my protector, so mired in his own pain he couldn't sense or acknowledge the physical and emotional pain he was causing. When he finally pulled away, the left side of my t-shirt was soaked with his tears.

Days later when Mom said she was leaving him, Dad came into my room. For the second time in my young life, Dad cried and hugged me. He begged me to talk to my Mom. "I love her, I can't live without her." No comfort for me, no thought for me, no love. "Tell her for me, she listens to you."

Later that day Mom told me we were going to take a vacation away from Dad. We were going to Canada ... where "Uncle Steve" lived ... so HE could take care of us. Mom recovering from a fractured skull. Mom who couldn't walk. Mom who shuffled around the house in a wheel chair. She and I (who could barely get up from bed) were going to have a great time.

She was smiling when she told me. We were going to be "best girl friends", we were going to take care of each other and have a fun vacation. I held my tears until she left my room.

No friends for Jeanne, no more physical therapy, no more church. What Mom didn't know, was that "Uncle Steve" had a new girl friend, so we couldn't stay with him.

I spent my entire summer vacation wheeling Mom up and down Vancouver streets. I spent months cooking and cleaning and shopping. I spent months listening to my Mom telling me what a wonderful time we were having together.

I spent months walking down Kingsway, looking into store windows and watching the cars pass by. I read the signs from the church across the way, advertising summer camp for kids. I saw children come and go, heard their laughter and longed to be a part of something that didn't involve pain and sorrow.

By the time we returned home to an empty house, my physical bruises were all but gone. My father was gone, most of the money was gone (sent to my Mom in Canada and used to pay for my Dad's tickets to Holland) and all the food was gone. My Mom and I ate whatever canned foods I could find.

When the food ran out Mom begged my newly married bother to pick up some food. Mom told me he didn't want to come (he eventually did). The internal bruises I suffered that long lonely summer, have never gone away.

I still get up at dawn … still pad around the house … still send mental hugs to its inhabitants. My parents are both long dead, along with my grandparents and uncles and aunts. My brother, gone forever from my life, left long ago to find his own salvation and grace.

When my father-in-law Mel still lived, I learned he loved 6am as well. "I'm a golfer" he had told me. "All golfers love the morning". Mel hated calling for tee off times at Lakeview on Fridays. He got a senior discount, but it took him hours to get through on the phone.

I made a deal to call for Mel. I had special speed dial and flash buttons on my phone. I programmed the phone number in my phone and sat pressing three buttons until I got through … usually in less than 30 minutes. For almost four years I got Mel's tee off times, on Friday mornings. I also fixed him lunches three days a week to take with him when he played golf.

Mel golfed three days a week for almost as long as I knew him. He won the senior championship at age 90, over folks 30 years younger he. His younger brother Quinton played with Mel the day he won. Quinn passed away that same evening, with a Cuban cigar in his hand. A few months later Mel had open heart surgery.

After Mel's open heart surgery he developed complications. He couldn't play golf. We'd often greet the morning together. I was relearning how to walk, (I'd been ill) and had started going out early in the morning with my walker. In 2007, Mel asked if he could walk with me. So I gave him my walker, purchased myself a cane, and we went out together.

When Mel was well enough to go outside, we walked up and down our street together. We enjoyed watching at the world spring to life around us. We'd comment on our neighborhood crows, Angel Stadium, weather, who was going to win this year's pennant, worms coming up from the ground and golf.

At some point Mel said he needed a break, and he'd sit down in my Hugo walker. When he was rested and ready to walk, he'd grab hold of my hand, or place one of his impossibly long arms across my back and squeeze. When Mel became too frail to walk outside, we'd walk inside the house, pausing occasionally to love a dog or a cat before returning to bed.

When Mel was ill, I'd lay down next to him, holding his hand until his pain passed and sleep took him. I can still feel the touch of his giant thumbnail pressing against my thumb.

Snapshots from a Broken Camera

Years earlier, when I first married Johnnie, I had been sick a lot. I explained to Mel I'd been told my symptoms were "all in my head." One day he looked at me and said, "Honey, anyone who says you're sick in the head is crazy. There's something physically wrong with you, and I'm going to help you get it taken care of." Mel found me doctors who eventually diagnosed my problems and helped find treatment.

Mel was the first family member who listened and heard me when I spoke. He was also the first father figure who really took care of me. When life was hard, or I cried, he held my hand and told me things would be OK. Mel never once hit me, never once insulted me, and never once called me crazy, lazy, stupid or selfish. It was through Mel I learned what true unconditional love felt like.

When the time came, I cared for Mel as I would have cared for my own father, had God given me that opportunity. I did everything I could to keep him safe, warm, healthy and loved. Mel called me his rock and his protector. The love Mel showed me was both my salvation and my grace. When he passed the best part of me went with him.

August 2007 ~ One last perfect Summer
Johnnie, Mel & Harvey on their regular evening walk

The Little Dutch Girl
Adopted by a Blue Eyed Crow

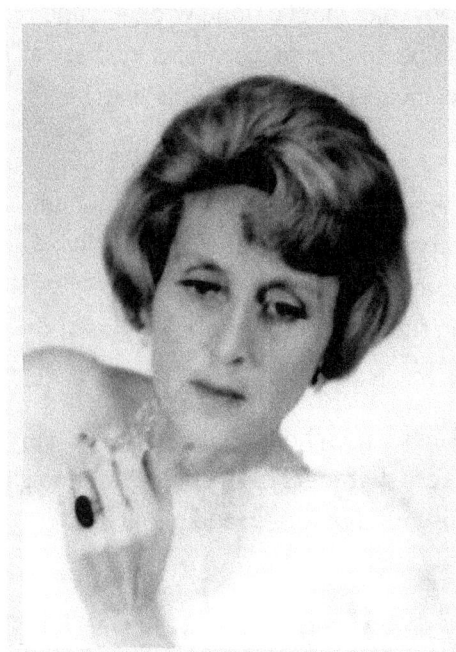

In ways that are difficult to explain ::: or understand ::: I grew up alone.

My Mom wasn't like other little girl's Moms. She was beautiful, intelligent, loving, cruel, brutal and unpredictable. What I didn't know or understand in those days ::: she was also bipolar and a paranoid schizophrenic.

When I was little she loved to dress me up. On good days ::: she told me I was her golden girl ::: her beautiful baby girl. On bad days ::: when I was sick or cried too much and she became overwhelmed ::: life could be ugly.

I grew up in Santa Ana California. 1960's Santa Ana wasn't anything like the huge city it is today.

Our home was located in what had originally been military housing. Our neighbors were squeaky clean, pure white ::: Americans through and through. Which meant my immigrant family stuck out like a sore thumb ::: even though we were white.

Snapshots from a Broken Camera

I started Kindergarten at age 4 ::: I was almost 2 years younger than most of the other children in my class. I remember my first day at school. Mom dressed me up ::: drove me to school ::: then dropped me off at class. No forewarning or explanations ::: she simply dumped me and walked off.

The problem was ::: whenever Mom was angry at me (which happened A LOT) she'd threaten to banish me to some far away school. Not knowing what I'd done wrong ::: and never having been away from home ::: I flew into a wild panic. The teacher held me back as I screamed and cried for my Mother. I remember feeling inconsolable grief while watching my Mom walk away ::: never stopping ::: never looking back.

Was small for my age ::: had long red hair, pale white skin, spoke with a Dutch accent and wore clothing from the Salvation Army. While elocution lessons (years later) eventually removed all traces of my accent ::: nothing could erase the fact my family was poor. So I became a target for the middle class "American" kids in their bright new Kenny Shoes and freshly pressed Sears outfits.

My first day of Kindergarten was hard ::: My first week in grade school was absolutely brutal. Some older kids invited me and a bunch of other first graders to the playground to sit on the Merry-Go-Round. I'd never been on a Merry-Go-Round before ::: and didn't know what to expect.

An older kid picked me up and placed me on the Merry-Go-Round ::: then said "Hold On" and laughed. The harder the big kids pushed the Merry-Go-Round ::: the faster it went. I could barely hold on ::: fear welled up inside me ::: I wanted to throw up. Suddenly I slid off the edge ::: landing underneath the Merry-Go-Round.

Every time I tried to get up my head hit the bottom of the rapidly spinning Merry-Go-Round ::: and I rolled around underneath. The children above me were kicking and screaming ::: their feet landing on my face, head and body. I screamed for what seemed an eternity ::: but the sound of my voice was drowned by the noise and laughter around me.

When the Merry-Go-Round stopped, a tall skinny boy with pitch black hair and vivid blue eyes picked me up from the ground. He looked at me with a worried face. "Are you OK?"

Stunned ::: I could only nod. "That's good, my name is Ray ::: Raymond Fredrick Patient. They did the same thing to me last year when I started first grade."

I was the only one of my family born in America ::: yet I still spoke with an accent ::: something I didn't realize until it was pointed out to me be a teacher. A few weeks later my parents were told I had a speech impediment (lazy tongue). The school said I needed "speech therapy". As this so called speech therapy was going to be on the school's dime ::: my Mom said OK. Thus started my weekly transformation into a true American via elocution lessons.

The area I grew up in was originally mostly farmland. There were bean and strawberry fields. There was a dairy farm down the street from my home ::: with lots of cows. Our backyard overlooked Raitt Street and seemingly endless bean fields. Sometimes on cool winter nights ::: when sound carried further ::: the rumble hum of occasional passing cars mirrored the sound the sea made as it crested on a distant shore. Some nights ::: when I was sad, scared or overwhelmed ::: I'd close my eyes focus on that sound ::: and fall asleep dreaming I was sailing out to sea.

Towards the end of Summer ::: when the beans were harvested ::: I remember the dozens of crows which came to feast on the freshly cut beans as they lay spread out upon the field to dry. I'd sit, my face pressed against our chain link fence watching the crows laugh and talk and soar high above my head.

A friend of my Dad called the crows tricksters. He told me stories his Grandfathers had told hIm when he was a boy. "A crow chooses the man ::: if he chooses you at birth he will never leave you." "How do you know if a crow chooses you?" I had asked. He just looked at me and smiled.

My Mom called crows thieves. "They like to steal shiny things and take them to their nest." "Why Mama?" I had asked She just looked at me and smiled.

The Autumn I turned 5, before the last of the bean fields were plowed over and seeded with cement to grow hundreds of houses ::: I sat silent, face pressed against the chain link fence ::: watching the crows each afternoon ::: hoping they would swoop down and play with me.

My friend Eileen was raped and killed that same Autumn ::: and buried alive near a new housing tract. Killed by the silent older boy who used to follow Eileen and me home from school. He had simply walked into her house ::: gone into to her room ::: then carried her from her home.

Snapshots from a Broken Camera

The night Eileen was killed I dreamt I saw ghosts at my window. I woke up my Mom and told her what I'd seen. She told me it was a dream ::: then looked at me and smiled. "Go to sleep."

The next morning I learned of Eileen's death. The police had found bits of her clothing near my bedroom window ::: snagged on a nail ::: along with some finger prints which turned out to be the boy's. He had come to take me as well ::: but all our doors and windows were locked.

That afternoon I lay down in the deep grass in our backyard ::: face pressed against the chain link fence ::: crying and watching the crows. I could hear the sound of them all around me, which made me cry more. My Mom had told me they were going to build houses over the rest of the fields. I loved looking at the open land ::: and feared for my beloved crows.

I heard an unfamiliar clicking noise next to me and looked up. A small crow ::: with the brightest blue eyes ::: was standing in the tall grass looking intently at me. She was so beautiful I wanted to reach out for her ::: but something held me back. So I sat ::: as still as I could ::: and simply watched.

Suddenly the sky above me was filled with dozens and dozens of crows. They were swooping and soaring ::: sitting on the chain link fence ::: and walking in the grass. A big crow walked up to the little crow next to me and made a loud "caw" sound. The little crow jumped up and landed awkwardly on my left shoulder.

Startled, I climbed quickly to my feet. As I did ::: the crows took flight around me ::: filling the air with the sound of their laughter. Head up ::: looking towards my friends ::: I began imitating their sounds. I stretched out my arms and twirled until I became so dizzy I fell down on the ground. As I lay on the ground ::: the little crow with the bright blue eyes ::: landed next to me one last time. She tugged once on my left sleeve then flew away.

The next time I saw my Dad's friend ::: I told him what had happened in my backyard. He looked at me and smiled. He said the crow had made me part of her family ::: that she and I would be friends forever.

The little crow with the bright blue eyes grew bigger ::: and her eyes grew dark. For almost 30 years ::: she returned to my backyard in the Summer and the Autumn. Ever fearless ::: she dived bombed our cats whenever she found them lounging in the grass. One memorable Autumn she returned and brought along two tiny crows with bright blue eyes ::: who grew into large dark eyed crows with little crows of their own.

I remember the afternoon I moved from my Santa Ana home ::: over 30 years after the little crow with the bright blue eyes had come into my life. My backyard was filled with her family and friends ::: dozens of crows ::: I looked at them one last time and then turned around. I was crying when we drove away.

I miss White Cloud ::: my Lakota teacher and grandfather ::: and the stories he told me of his life in the plains. I miss Ray F. Patient (my grade school savior and best friend) who walked me home from school every day after Eileen's murder. Ray encouraged me to be an artist ::: to draw ::: to sing ::: to write. Ray died of AIDS in the 80s. Most of all I miss the little crow with the bright blue eyes who chose me ::: and allowed me to be part of her family.

Easter:
A time for Gratitude and Renewal

A Story about Friendship

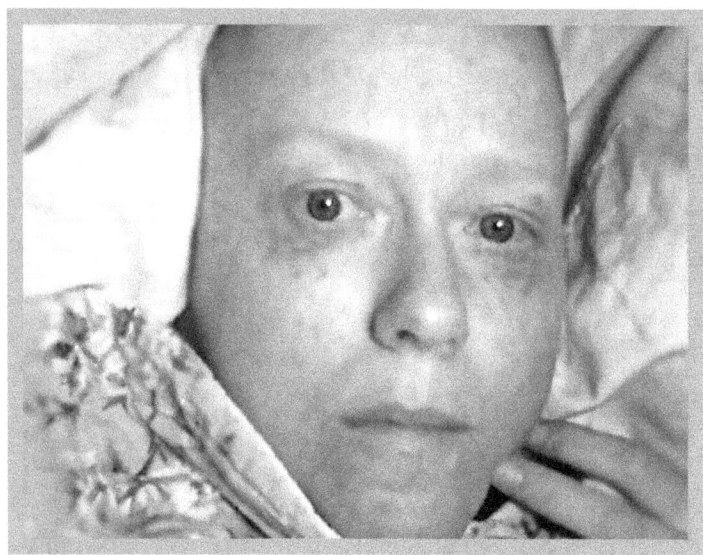

In June of 2005 I'd just been released from ICU. I could barely walk, I bald and looked like hell, I'd feel faint and my heart hammered every time I stood up ::: I didn't know why. It would be five more years before I learned I have Dysautonomia ::: and how to live with it.

Insanely worried, and stressed practically to the point of immobility ::: I sat down at my piano and played. Fruit-loop that I am ::: I got the wild idea to videotape myself while playing. I was bald at the time ::: which should give an idea of how much of a fruit-loop.

I mean what type of crazy woman would videotape herself after all her hair fell out?!

Eventually I merged photos, and a song I wrote for Cameron into a sort'a kind'a video thank you note. Cameron Charles Switzer ::: a musician / welder ::: who saved my life.

I met Cameron Switzer almost a decade ago. We were both into music and corresponded on the web a long time before meeting and becoming friends.

In 2004, I'd told my family I wanted to die. No more hospitals ::: no more doctors ::: no more fear. In February of that year, when I was near death Cameron showed up at my home ::: he later told me he'd had a bad feeling.

He'd driven well over an hour to my house ::: where he found me alone unconscious on the floor of my office. He packed a bag ::: told my husband I was NOT going to die ::: and took me to his home. That night he literally saved my life when I went into respiratory arrest.

Cameron cared for me for almost 9 months, helping me relearn how to walk, sit up and move around ::: without terror welling up inside me.

Cameron set up my keyboard next to my bed and encouraged me to sit up and play. At first I could only play a few minutes at a time. Gradually as my strength and stamina returned ::: he pushed my physical limits even further ::: encouraging me to perform (with him) as a member of the Los Angeles Scottish Fiddlers. (The most amazing group people I've ever met)

Eventually Cameron also helped me reconnect with the technical part of music, and encouraged me to start composing again ::: the old fashioned way. It was because of Cameron I again learned to read and write music.

While Cameron is no longer a part of my life, I will be forever grateful for having known him.

Cameron and I performing together at his 50's birthday Party.

❧Once Upon a Time in America

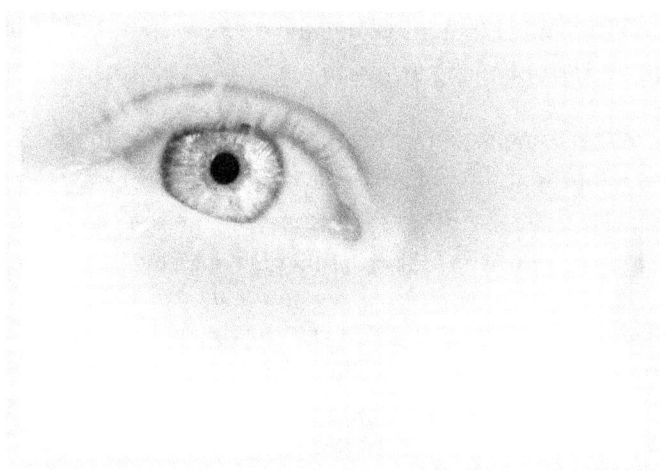

Once upon a time, when the world was still young, I believed that the spiritual among us didn't have it in them to lie, steal, or harm others ::: that God always protected his children, and trusted that good always triumphed over evil.

I was born sick and frail, and believed the broken portions of my body were one of God's special gifts. In invitation for me to look deeper for the good in ALL life. My journey towards Grace, that indefinable something which brought me closer to God ::: the Divine in life ::: came during small moments when my spirit managed to transcend my body.

Over the years I have mostly stool silent during hurt, pain and chaos life sent my way ::: taking it on the chin ::: believing these trials would eventually end ::: the clouds would part ::: and life would eventually be good.

I have had some stellar moments ::: moments of peace, contentment, hope, faith and love. There have been so many strange coincidences in my life ::: that said ::: I don't believe in coincidence.

As a respiratory therapist, I held the hand of the doctor who birthed me ::: the man who deftly brought me into this world ::: comforting him as he passed from this existence.   I did CPR on both my father and uncle as their lives faded away. I comforted hundreds of people as they made their final journey from this planet ::: the memory of each person's end is etched upon my soul.

I sat next to Bill Hill (keyboardist to the Platters) and felt the vibration his hands made as they raced along the piano keys. Memorizing each motion and each sound ::: the laughter of his voice as he taught me (a small red headed child) how to play "riffs".

The first time I sang on key in the church sanctuary at age 11 ::: my voice transcending vocal scars left after decades of illness. The first time I sang on stage ::: the first time I sang on the radio ::: the first time I sang on television. So many dreams ::: so many hopes.

I gave up my dreams of being an artist to follow my Mom's dreams that I enter the medical field. So I sang to my patients in ICU/CCU ::: years before radios and televisions were allowed. I sang in the darkness to anyone willing to listen. Mostly ::: I sang alone.

When I was almost 30, my oldest and dearest friend ::: the one who reminded me constantly "you were born an artist" died of AIDS. His death reminded me how far off course I'd gone. I returned to school, returned to writing, returned to music ::: eventually earning an embarrassment of awards ::: just as my friend had foretold a lifetime before.

Yet the healer wasn't that easy to discard. For the better part of a decade I cared for my Mom ::: mostly unaided and alone. Difficult time to describe, as my Mom wasn't a particularly kind or easy person to be related to. My Mom wasn't someone you could ever really know ::: she was basically someone you survived.

Yet I loved her with an intensity difficult to describe ::: let alone define. Hope was always in my heart ::: hope she would one day love me completely, a love unequivocal and unconditional ::: for all that I was, had been, and would be.

Sadly ::: the sicker Mom became ::: the harsher she became. When I didn't give her what she wanted, I was called a prick, a cunt or a bitch. Had she been able to rip my soul from my body and replace it with her own ::: and live through me ::: she would have quickly cast me aside and done so ::: never looking back.

I loved my Mother unconditionally, because I believed this was what God expected. I believed I wouldn't be worthy of unconditional love if I wasn't willing to give it myself. So I fed her when she was hungry, soothed her when she was ill, comforted her when she was sad, and let her know she was special (to me) and needed (by me) and would never be alone.

Grace came three months prior to my Mother's death ::: when she held me in her arms and told me she loved me ::: was proud of me ::: and begged forgiveness for all the pain she had caused.

Snapshots from a Broken Camera

We talked for hours on end ::: each day becoming a lifetime. We knew one and other so well we could finish each other's sentences. We spoke about family members past ::: about life ::: details both mundane and divine. We were friends then ::: between her rages and revelations ::: living an eternity in three all too brief months :::: then she died.

I gave thanks to God I hadn't been with my Mother when she died. Overwhelmed with guilt, I prayed forgiveness for my selfish need to not see her passing. The confusion of it all crushed me. The brutality of finding myself completely and totally without family ::: suddenly old ::: mind numbingly poor ::: inches away from living on the street ::: hungry ::: cold ::: achingly alone ::: tore at my soul and twisted all I believed until my thoughts had become wild alien and barely recognizable.

I have been broken ::: my body :::: and gradually my soul ::: for a very long time. I've held too many people as they died ::: comforted too many people as they lay ill ::: and lost myself to the process. Ironically, as crazy as it must sound, I didn't believe I had a choice. You see I was brought up to never, EVER say no.

I'd been told ::: and always believed ::: if I lived right, did God's work ::: when the time came :::: there would be someone there to love and aid me ::: as I had loved and aided others. So I've tried to be strong ::: to grow beyond fear and pain ::: into a person worthy of God's grace.

A few years after my Mom died I married. I was blessed to be part of a warm and loving family. When my husband's mother was dying of cancer ::: I helped as much as this family would allow. Years later, when my husband's father became ill :::: I was grateful to be his caregiver (as he had been for me). When my husband's brother was diagnosed with terminal cancer ::: we took him into our home for hospice.

I held both the Father and the Son as they lay dying. I have seen enough sorrow and death to last a thousand lifetimes. Now I struggle with the memories of a lifetime of hurt and sorrow and pain and illness. Memories of those I've loved are intermingled and tangled up with the memories of my abusers.

There's a palpable sorrow, difficult to define, within each breath I take. Always there, sometimes just below the surface, sometimes pounding in my brain, sometimes locked within the hammering of my heart ::: it NEVER leaves me.

Papa Papa, Where are you Papa

When I'm home alone, the toddler locked within my body pushes to get out. Her screams emanating from my mouth and my body, are enmeshed in HER memories, NOT mine. Yet the intensity of what she feels overwhelms me and I am lost, so I weep with her. Together we wander through my empty home, both calling out for Papa. He never answers.

The Death of Thomas Johnson
~ Two Years Later

Thursday, April 7, 2011

Today Marks the 2 year anniversary of my Brother-in-Law Tom's Death. It also marks the 1 year anniversary of the day my Husband Johnnie was diagnosed with Melanoma. The irony being that Tom died of stage IV Melanoma.

Johnnie discovered his tumor while being treated for a pit bull attack. I guess life is just full of irony. Tom waited 17 years to see a doctor about the lump in his neck and eventually died. Johnnie started treatment ASAP and is still with us. A year and multiple outpatient surgeries later, Johnnie remains cancer free.

I'm fat, which to a lot of people is the same as being worthless and ugly. Doesn't matter I'm smart and talented ... they can't hear me, and when these people look at me ... all they see is FAT. My brother-in-law Tom was one of those people.

The day my future brother-in-law Tom learned I was going to marry his brother he took it upon himself to drive to my home. He didn't want me to marry his then 46-year-old brother.

He came with a basket full of reasons why I should leave Johnnie. Tom said (1) it was too soon after the death of his Mother, (2) Johnnie hadn't yet dated enough women, (3) Johnnie needed another type of woman (translation: NOT FAT LIKE YOU), and (4)that there's no way Johnnie would have thought of marrying had "I" not put the idea in his head. (For the record Johnnie asked me, not the other way around).

 I told Tom I loved Johnnie but I wasn't desperate, if Johnnie told me he didn't want to get married I'd leave him alone. The thing is, Johnnie wanted to get married and was righteously pissed off at his Brother for suggesting otherwise.

When we got past Tom's polite BS, the simple truth was he didn't think me good enough, successful enough or attractive enough to be in HIS family.

He refused to come to our wedding. And for the entire time we were married, until the time he was diagnosed with malignant melanoma, he took every opportunity to make my life a living hell.

I'm not going to write about the things Tom did to hurt me, or drive Johnnie and I apart, other than to say he very nearly succeeded.

In 2003 I moved out for six months, and returned only after Mel developed health problems. Johnnie and I cared for Mel - unassisted by Tom - until his death five years later.   Three months after Mel died, Tom moved in to do hospice in our home. We cared for him until his death, another three months later.

Tom and I talked a lot during his last days. We talked about the weather, about movies, cooking, about the crazy things he'd done over the years, and how sad it was that we'd never been friends.

Ever the opinionated bitch, I told him that was his fault. He looked at me with sad eyes and answered, "I know I know".

I'm not sure if it was the all pain medication making him chatty, or what. He apologized to me and begged Johnnie's forgiveness for a lot of bad stuff he'd done. It was a heartbreaking time for the everyone.

Tom died a slow, agonizing and painful death. Prior to his passing, I wondered if I had it in me to comfort and/or hold him when he died. Some of the wounds were still to raw and painful ... the past too close.

When told he was dying, Tom's beloved x-girlfriend Kris came and stayed at the house. Amazingly Tom rallied and came back to life. After a week of no food, Tom ate everything Kris gave him, drank fluids, and seemed to rally. She called her family and all their friends who also came and sat with Tom. Our home was filled with Tom's friends. Kris took amazing and loving care of Tom. Sadly Tom was still dying. Dying by inches at a time. After two weeks Kris needed to take care of a few work related things.

I'll never forget the day Tom died. Kris had to leave. I worked in the medical field for the better part of two decades, so I knew the signs. I told Kris I thought Tom only had a few hours. But then I'd told her Tom was dying two weeks ago ... and he kept coming back.

About a half hour after Kris left the house, Tom's breathing became labored and rapid. I talked with Tom and held his hand, the fear in his eyes filled me with a type of sadness I've never known.

Snapshots from a Broken Camera

Over the years I've stood vigil to hundreds of deaths ... just part of my job. I also did CPR on both my Dad and Uncle when they each succumb to heart disease. But I've never seen a death like Tom's.

As ordered, I put a 0.5mg Ativan (not a large dose, just enough to help calm) under his tongue and told Tom to try and relax. I called Johnnie into the room and told him it was time. I left a message on Kris' phone.   As Tom lay dying, Johnnie scooped him up in his arms and talked to him. For the better part of an hour Johnnie kept talking with Tom. He was talking with Tom when his breathing stopped.

I was telling Tom to relax and not be afraid ... to let go. He was looking at me and crying. When it was over I was amazed to find myself laying on the bed beside Tom, cradling his hand in mine. Something I hadn't thought myself capable of.

I don't know if my presence gave Tom any sort of comfort during his death, I only know I'm glad I was able to try.

The Johnson Family men in better days
Johnnie Johnson, Mel Johnson, Quinton Johnson, Tom Johnson

Sticks and Stones and Words all hurt

Copy of Blog published in July 2011

On July 3rd I got some twitters asking me to send an email to Sheila Polk (Arizona DA) about my experiences with James Arthur Ray. It was absolutely the last thing I wanted to do. I talked to my husband and asked him what his opinion was. He said he thought I'd regret not writing it, so "you'd better get busy".

I tried writing on Saturday, but cried every time I attempted to put into words how my one and only meeting with James Arthur Ray had affected me ::: still affects ::: me. To this day I still can't completely wrap my brain around the why part.

I just feel so damned stupid. I mean what kind of a person becomes rabidly suicidal at the words of a stranger?! They're ONLY words, but they still hurt ::: and that simple fact fills me with hopelessness and shame.

I can't write in a letter how much energy and effort it took for me to attend My Ray's free event. On days like today, I can barely walk ::: can't raise my arms above my head ::: can barely brush my hair up in a ponytail, let alone get dressed easily. On days like today ::: I talk to the cat, play with our greyhounds, cry, pray, watch old movies and pretend I don't hurt.

On days like today my closest friends are the reflections of Doris Day or Jack Lemon on my HD TV. I laugh at their antics and try to imagine what it would feel like to be back in a simpler time ::: in a world I understood much better than the world I now live in.

Allergies force me to live my separate from almost everyone else. I'm like a person locked inside a building with a big picture window ::: watching the world go on around me ::: seeing but never being seen or touched.

 Lord how James Arthur Ray filled me with Hope ::: that's the thing I'm most ashamed by ::: that I could be so hungry for health ::: a hand up ::: a pat on the back ::: someone to help me find a better healthier life ::: that I became a total idiot sap and bought into his con.

In 2007, when James Arthur Ray looked at me with total disdain, it reminded me of all the people who've judged me by my outward appearance and found me wanting. When James

Snapshots from a Broken Camera

Arthur Ray said I'd never be anything but a looser and a fat slob ::: it was as if he'd brought forward my worst fears and my shame at how illness had shaped my body.

I could write a thousand concertos, record countless songs, publish more stories, photos, win awards, etc. ::: but nothing, absolutely nothing I could accomplish in this world would ever change the view people like James Arthur Ray have of people who look like me.

It's been four years since I met James Ray. Four years later and I still have nightmares, and still cringe at the thought attending a public event. How stupid is that?

The thing is, I'm just one of who knows how many nameless faceless people who have crossed James Ray's path. How many other people has he pushed into despair with his words?

Which brings me to another question that's been bothering me ::: what really happened to Colleen Conaway? What did he say (he was with her moments before she jumped / was pushed) to cause such a tragic end. Why did he lie about it afterward? Why the cover up? Why wasn't he charged?

Why is James Arthur Ray able to steal millions -- commit corporate fraud and grand theft -- and be allowed to use that money to fund one of the most despicable defenses I've ever seen?

Why is it legal for Munger Tolles and Olson (ANY LAW FIRM) to accept money from such a questionable source ::: without any legal ramifications?!!

Why is James Arthur Ray walking free after being found GUILTY? Where is the justice for the people he killed or permanently maimed?

I'm tired, don't feel well and I'm rambling ... sorry about that. This whole trial thing has really got me down.

I spent most of the 4th writing a letter to Polk. I spell checked it and then sent it before I could chicken out and delete it. I've had horrid nightmares every night since. I've pasted a copy of it below for anyone who's interested.

For the record I didn't write it for me ::: I intend to find my own salvation ::: grace ::: hope. I wrote it in the hopes it might help keep James Arthur Ray from ever having the power to hurt ANYONE again ::: EVER!

Sheila Polk, SBN 007514
County Attorney
255 East Gurley Street, 3rd Floor
Prescott , AZ 86301

phone: (928) 771-3344
email: ycao@co.yavapai.az.us

Ms Polk:

You and I have never met.

I am part of a group of a hundred or so people who have been following the James Arthur Ray trial via the Internet (blogger, twitter, CNN Live, Facebook, etc.). I received some twitters this morning from [NancyOgilvie] and [@La_Huesera La Vaughn] asking me to send my story to you.

I had hoped once the trial was over and Mr. Ray was found guilty ... I could put my memories of him away and go on with my life, secure in the knowledge that Mr. Ray's words or actions would never again cause anyone harm. Now I'm being told there's a real chance that Mr. Ray may only get probation ... and he may eventually start over doing the same things he did in the past.

This is a difficult letter for me to write. Even now, four years after the event, I still have nightmares about what transpired. To this day I struggle to understand why a man I had never met or had any contact with would verbally assault me in front of a room full of strangers.

My husband and I met James Arthur Ray at the Anaheim Marriott on May 31, 2007, while attending one of his free seminars. (please see attached email invitation and link posted immediately below)

Orange County, CA:

May 31, 2007 at 7:00 PM
Event Location:
Marriott Anaheim
700 West Convention Way
Anaheim, CA 92802

Snapshots from a Broken Camera

I'm currently disabled and have been on SSDI since about 1990. I suffer from Tourettes, fibromyalgia, celiac disease, Dysautonomia (causes labile blood pressure and cardiac arrhythmia) and degenerative bone disease, along with severe food and chemical sensitivities/allergies. I was confined to a wheelchair for a while, nowadays I walk with a cane or walker.

Prior to becoming disabled I had a successful career. I've been listed in "Who's Who of American Women since 1991, I'm also listed in "Who's Who in America" and "Who's Who in the World". My illustrations, graphics, photographs and stories have been published internationally and garnered me numerous awards. I'm also a published composer/musician.

I've learned people (like James Ray) often judge other's by how they look, how much money they have, what they do, who they know, etc.. Which is the main reason I mentioned who I used to be, awards I've won, and what I used to do before I became too ill to live a normal life.

When the Secret came out I was initially put off by it. That said, I'm ashamed to admit that after hearing Oprah rave about the Secret, I allowed myself to get caught up in all that baloney. I respected Oprah's opinion so much I purchased the CD. By the time I purchased the book I was a woman on a quest.

I read eventually read Mr. Ray's book "The Science of Success", and signed up for emails from James Ray International. I began walking more (a good thing), making affirmations (a silly thing), and in general making a fool of myself (a sad thing). When I received an invitation to one of his free events taking place a few blocks from my home, I signed up my husband and myself (a really stupid thing).

I had wanted to hear Mr. Ray speak and thank him for reminding me I'm more than my body.

To understand what a big deal this was for me you need to understand how sick I'd been, how difficult it was (and is for me to get around) and how little I get out. This was the first time in years I attended a public event. The first time in years I went someplace public without wearing a special mask (w/ activated carbon filters). The first time in years stood in line for hours (they started the event 2 hours late).

My husband and I sat close to the front, at the end of an aisle, so I could keep my walker next to me. We watched and listened to Mr. Ray speak about his life, how poor he'd been, how he made himself over. We heard stories of people who had healed completely or became rich after reading his books, listening to his CDs and attending his seminars.

Towards the end of the event, Mr. Ray told everyone to pick up the packet of information we'd been given at the front door. He told us to fill out the contract for an upcoming seminar without thinking. "Say yes, do it now, before you change your mind. Don't worry about the money. The money will come once you sign up."

My husband was nudging me to fill it in. We were too broke, and I didn't feel right borrowing from his father. I already owed him money for special medications I'd been taking. I read the small print and saw Mr. Ray's so called iron clad refund policy was meaningless. He kept talking and saying "if you sign up today, you can bring someone with you for free." So we asked a JRI employee if they carried their own paper, that I'd pay them off monthly. The answer was no. It was for our own good, so we could learn how to make money on our own.

The person I spoke with spent 30 minutes trying to talk me into signing for something I couldn't afford. Telling me not to worry and that the money would come to pay for it. I told them about my allergy problems, and they said I'd be fine. "No one ever got sick at a James Ray event. People get better."

In the end we decided not to sign up for the events they were selling that day. We didn't have the $10,000 they were ultimately asking for, not counting transportation, hotel rooms, food, books, CDs ,etc. I'm ashamed to admit, had they offered to carry their own paper, or given us the means to pay them back over time ... we'd have signed up without question. But they didn't ... and we were broke, and I wasn't willing to legally bind myself to something I knew I couldn't afford.

There must have been a couple of thousand people at this event. It seemed like they were all signing up for future seminars. We felt as if something really important and life altering had just passed us by. I reminded my husband that my main reason for attending this even was to thank Mr. Ray for reminding me I'm more than my body, and to give him a small gift.

Mr. Ray was at the end of the room talking with dozens of people, hundreds more waiting to speak with him. Every so often he would look away from the crowd, a bored expression on his face. Then he'd step forward to the next person and flash this on-demand smile of his.

As I made my way up the isle toward Mr. Ray he flashed me an expression that bordered on disgust. I've seen that look before, from so called beautiful people who are offended by the sight of fat or disabled people. Semi bald (my hair occasionally falls out when I'm sick), pale and bloated from my allergies, overweight and walking with the aid of a walker, I was a natural target for mean spirited people.

One of the reasons I didn't get out much in those days was because I knew how bad I looked. At best people would stare at me or come up and ask me how long I'd been on chemo ... at worst people would point at me and snicker.

I asked my husband if he'd seen Mr. Ray flash me a strange look. He shook his head and shrugged, then asked me if it was possible I was over thinking things. So I decided to stay in line and wait to speak with Mr. Ray.

When I reached out to shake Mr. Ray's hand he looked at me, reached for my husband's hand and then crossed his arms. When I started to thank Mr. Ray, I spoke five words ... at which point he interrupted me to ask if we'd signed up for any of his seminars.

When I started telling him we had no money and were unable to attend, he again interrupted me.

James Ray

"I'm going to do you a favor" he said, "Don't ever say that again, [that you don't have money] the universe is listening."

Me

"But I don't have any money right ... (I was going to say right now)"

James Ray ... interrupting again ... now shouting

"I TOLD YOU NOT TO SAY THAT!"

Me

"But it's true."

James Ray ... shouting even more loudly

"Then borrow it!"

Me

"I have no one to borrow from."

James Ray ... speaking in a loud and angry tone

"You mean to say your life is so miserable that you have absolutely no friends who can loan you money?"

Me ... quietly

"No, my friends are struggling to."

James Ray ... shouting

"You'll never be anything but a fat slob and looser if you don't attend my retreat."

The brutality of his words, the sound of his voice, the anger in its tone took my breath away. I think some of the people standing next to me were shocked by his words, but in reality I don't know.

If I live to be a 100, I'll never forget what Mr. Ray did next. He looked at me and smiled, a hard cold angry smile that chilled me to the bone. Then Mr. Ray walked away from me and motioned to the woman standing behind me.

When she came forward, he put his arm around her and turned on a 200 watt smile as her friend took a picture of the two of them together.

Whispers from people around me

"Did he just call that woman with the walker a fat slob?" "What did she say?" "Look at that lard assed bitch, James is right, she's nothing ... a nobody."

Snapshots from a Broken Camera

All I wanted to do at that point is run. But I'm disabled and was lucky to get around with my walker. So I waddled out of the conference room in a slow shuffle, surrounded by strangers, struggling to hold back tears. While making my way to the parking structure all I could think about was finding the highest part and jumping off. Please know I've never reacted this strongly to anyone's words!

I doubt if I will ever understand why Mr. Ray spoke to me the way he did, let alone why I reacted the way I did. I cried for weeks afterward. To this day I don't know why the words of a stranger filled me with so much hopeless despair, that for months afterward all I could think of was ending my life.

While I know autoimmune disease will eventually kill me, I'm going to struggle to stay alive for as long as physically possible. I've come to terms with my illness and the day to day pain that comes with it. I try to take each day as it comes, and strive to live my life as fully and completely as physically possible. Some days are better than others. I live for the good days.

I'm writing to you now for the others Mr. Ray has harmed ... both by his words and his actions. I don't believe I'm the only person he has treated this badly ... because his words seemed too easy and too practiced.

I can't help wondering how many other people gave up on life, or worse yet, committed suicide because of something he said or did. I only know I'm appalled at how close I came to ending my own life the day I met Mr. Ray.

Please don't let Mr. Ray hurt any more people. If he doesn't get jail time and there are no ramifications for his actions, I'm afraid he keep doing bad things.

Thank you for taking the time to read this.

Sincerely,

Jeanne Barkemeijer de Wit

Jeanne Barkemeijer de Wit

Views On Loosing a brother

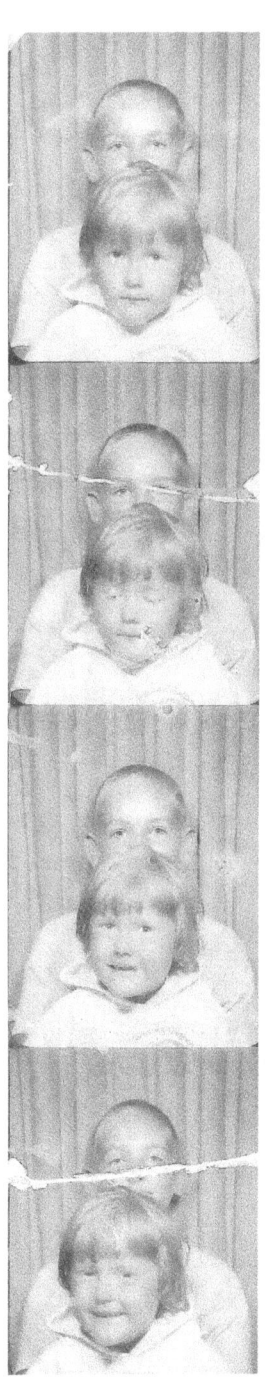

I grew up believing my brother Dick was a God. Incredibly smart, multi-talented and good looking, he was everything I aspired to but knew I could never be. Concert violinist, world class photographer, brilliant student, surfer, guitarist, and general all around cool guy.

Whenever I had trouble with math, or spelling or ANY school project I'd hear how great my brother was ... and how stupid I am.

Mom to me at age 6 ...

"You can't do simple arithmetic?! Your brother does advanced Algebra! Why can't you be more like Dick?"

"You can't do your multiplication tables?! God you're stupid! In Holland I had them ALL memorized by the time I was six!"

My brother AND my Mom could do EVERYTHING better than me. What kid could compete with that much talent? Looking back now, my brother's 7 years old than I am, and my mom was 36 years older, so I was being set up for failure.

At age six I gave up and accepted the fact of my stupidity.

I adored my brother, any attention he gave me was like a gift. I loved the fact that this amazing person was "MY" brother. I always wanted to be around him. I'm sure he thought me a royal pain in the tush.

The summer I turned four, I got a hold of one of Dick's old swimming trunks. I thought if I wore them without a girl's swimming top, I could will myself into a boy. I had really short hair at the time, and a number of the neighbors thought I was a boy, which only served to fuel my fantasy.

One morning while speeding down the sidewalk in my tricycle, I landed in our neighbor's rose bushes. I ran into the house, crying my eyes out. As my Mom pulled the thorns out one by one, she told me I wouldn't have been hurt as bad if I'd been wearing a top or blouse.

Snapshots from a Broken Camera

From that day on I always wore a top.

My brother's bedroom and mine were connected by a bathroom in the middle. I loved peering into my brother's room from our adjacent bathroom. His room was full of interesting looking books, models he'd made, neat toys and other fascinating things.

For a while he got into keeping aquariums. My Dad built a floor to ceiling wall of shelves to hold all Dick's fish tanks. I loved the sound the pumps made at night, and the pretty colors of all the fish when the lights were on.

My Brother and I

My brother was the best part of my childhood, the person I most admired and believed in. I felt safe when he was around, and proud that we were related. I would have done anything for him and defended him with my life.

In 1969, when my brother turned 21, (back in the days when you had to be 21 to be considered an adult) he moved out of the house. He and our Mother did not get along. That's sort of an understatement actually. His life at home was a living hell. Both of ours were.

I understood why he needed to leave, and was happy for him. I hoped and prayed one day he would come back to rescue me from hell. I was 13 at the time. My brother never came to my rescue. And although I've tried in so many ways to have a close relationship with my brother, from that day on he's always kept me at arm's length.

From time to time, between marriages and jobs, Dick's dropped into my life for a day or a week or a month. He took me to a Star Trek movie after he divorced his second wife Linda, which really blew my mind. In the end he's always returned to keeping me at distance.

He married two of my friends, is still married to one. Used my car for a year, took jobs I helped him get ... but was still mostly unreachable. At which point I assumed it was me.

When I recommended him to work with me at D-Link I agreed to no wage increases while he was there. Something I only told my Father. I remember when a coworker made fat jokes about me, that my brother always laughed with him. One day my Dad had been there when they were joking about me, and found me crying at my desk.

Dad to me ...

"Do you want me to talk to your brother? You know he doesn't mean it."

Me to Dad ...
"What's the point? I am fat. And yes he does mean it. Even if he didn't start the conversation, he certainly finished it "

Dad to Me ...

"You're not *that* fat Shrimpy (his pet name for me) and you're not ugly." he gave me one of his patented bone crushing bear hugs. "So stop crying."

My Dad was dying at the time, and I knew it. Long story that. Yet he still took the time to see his kids at work. He died a month later, at home in his bed. The day before he died, Dad came to the office to take my brother and I to lunch. My brother begged off.

They day my Mom gave my brother the keys to my Dad's VW it felt as if Dad died again. He was so much a part of that car. I hadn't cried when Dad died, but cried while preparing the car for my brother. After Dick left with Dad's car I cried for hours on end. For years afterward, I cried every time I heard a Volkswagen drive down our street.

Within days of Dad's death, my brother moved to Colorado. That was over 21 years ago. I've seen him once since, when Mom died in 1994.

Snapshots from a Broken Camera

For a while I wrote letters, which he rarely answered. Eventually I wrote his wife Angie, who always answered. Mom became too sick and I had to quit my job to care for her. My health started going downhill. Mom died, and I was in and out of hospitals. Some days I had little or nothing to eat, I got food from a local non profit ... it was a bleak time.

My car broke down, and the breaks needed fixing. The owner of the gas station I'd been going to for the past 15 years said he'd repair it for free. He said your my family had been good customers and he liked my Dad. Amazing kindness and the darkest of moments.

Through all the times in my life ... good, bad, indifferent ... I'd always believed that one day my brother and I would connect again as family. He was, and still is, the person I most admire in life. There's not a day that goes by when I don't miss him.

On January 6, 2010 I found my Brother on Facebook. I was overjoyed. I immediately sent a friend request and hoped this could be a new beginning for us. Eight hours later his Facebook page had been taken down. A day or so later he emailed me, saying he was busy but would get back to me soon.

Jean,

Good to hear from you. Sorry about Facebook, but it is just not my thing. Got talked into joining and it has been way over the top.

Who are these people! I'll send you an other email soon.

Dick

~ The promised email never arrived ~

The whole Facebook thing really threw me for a loop, I cried constantly afterward. I hadn't expected that sort of response, and ruminated about it for days. Two sentences kept repeating over and over in my brain "Why doesn't he like me?" and "What did I do wrong?"

After a week of crying to the point of dehydration, near constant melt downs and acting like a total fool, I decided to write a letter to my brother. Fearing the worst, no response or bad response ... I had the mother of all panic attacks and ended up in E.R. with tachycardia and a blood pressure of 230/200.

I don't want anyone to think I went over the deep end because of what my brother did or didn't say. As that's not the case.

Last year I watched my father-in-law (and dearest friend) die ... followed six months later by my brother-in-law Tom's death to stage IV melanoma in our home. (He did hospice)

Not that we were close, but Tom's death affected me deeply. It forced me to look at the distance between my own brother and myself. Facing so many losses in such a short period of time, really messed with my mind.

So armed with a soul shattering need for answers ... and bolstered by a healthy dose of Lorazepam (supplied by an understanding Kaiser Permanente E.R. doctor) I finished my letter and sent it out.

Trying to Reconnect for the Last Time

Sun, Jan24, 2010 at 5:40PM,
Jeanne Barkemeijer de Wit wrote:

Dearest Dick:

It's been way too many years since either one of us have spoken, let alone kept in touch in anything other than a cursory manor. So much time has passed, I wonder if either one of us would recognize the other if we happened to pass on the street. I don't understand why there's no real connection between the two of us.

I don't understand why you disconnected the phone number you gave me years ago, and never gave me a new one, let alone call. While it may be coincidental, it felt really weird to have you shut down your Facebook page immediately after receiving my friend request. I don't understand why you never acknowledge gifts, respond to letters or answer my emails ... other than to say you're busy and you'll get back to me ... which of course you never do.

If you no longer desire further contact, I can obviously live with that, as that's more or less the way things have felt like to me for a very long time. But could you please get that message across honestly and directly. Simply tell me to stop trying to contact you and I promise you'll never hear from me again. If you still want to know your sister, that's great."

I remember you as the best part of a phenomenally screwed up and painful childhood. You were the person I always looked up to, admired, and wished I could be like. Whenever I felt life was hopeless, I took solace in the knowledge that everything I believed good in our family, resided in you. I'd love the opportunity to get to know that person again. Because I've really missed having him in my life.

Snapshots from a Broken Camera

If you and Ange need a rest, and if the idea of reconnecting with the weird side of your family intrigues you ... we own a really large house with extra rooms and all the amenities, all geared to tall people.

(Including three state of the art Sony Bravia digital HD televisions, extra large sofas, chairs, and beds, ultra high speed Internet, wireless WAN/LAN, multiple computers, enclosed 10 person Jacuzzi, tricked out patio, tons of software, musical instruments, cameras etc., and more) If you're interested in a reunion and/or you'd also like to see Dirk ... I'll gladly send tickets for the both of you to fly over to OC. You can stay as little or as long as you wish.

Regardless of your decision, please don't blow me off or tell me you're too busy to respond. That excuse was old 10 years ago. So please let me know, one way or another, where the two of us stand, and if I need to stop contacting you.

Love Always,
Jeanne"

On Wed, Jan 27, 2010 at 8:30 AM, Dick Barkemeijer de Wit wrote:

Just a quick note. My pc crashed. Have gone over to a friend's house to use their computer. Just wanted to let you know I haven't forgotten about you. Not putting you off. No outside computer access at work and I'll be in training for the next three days and working on Sat. Hope to have a working pc late Sun. Get back to you as soon as I can. Hope you understand. Have to go, long drive to the training center."

~ as before, the promised email never arrived ~

Thu, Mar 11, 2010 4:22PM,
Jeanne Barkemeijer de Wit wrote:

Dick:

I hope you're OK.

While I may just be restating the obvious, I've finally gotten it through my head that you don't want a relationship or contact with me. I wish I knew why in the hell that is, but it's kind'a clear you're never going to share that info with me.

Truth be told I'm tired of waiting for a response from you (good bad or indifferent). Life's too damned short to be spent waiting for something that never comes.

That said, I won't be bothering you with emails or letters any more. My love and good wishes go to you and Angie both. I hope life grants you only good things.

Love and Care, sis

Thus ended decades of trying to get close to the person I loved most in my immediate family.

~ To date I haven't receive any type of response from my brother ~

~ I no longer expect one ~

For decades I've always thought there was something wrong with me, that my brother was ashamed of me, how I looked, or that something I'd said, not said, done, or didn't do properly, caused the distance to widen between us.

The way things now stand, I have no relationship with my brother. In reality, I haven't had one in decades. I've been living in a dream for more years than I care to say. A dream where I had a brother who cared about me as much as I cared about him.

Now that I'm forced to accept that no relationship exists between my brother and myself, it feels as if he died. I feel homeless and adrift. I still love my brother, and I miss him more than I have words to express. I always will.

I remember my brother as tall, good looking, wildly talented, funny, witty and impossibly smart. I'll always think of him as the coolest person I ever knew, and the best part of my childhood. I'm grateful for having had him in my life, if even for a brief time.

God willing, one day, my brother (or someone he knows) will take the time to tell me why he chose to exile me from his life.

Snapshots from a Broken Camera

UPDATE ~ December 2012-April 2013

Don't know why, but something kept urging me to call my sister-in-law. Something was wrong, I'd dreamt she was ill and I wanted to hear her voice. I spent weeks trying to locate an address other than their post office box. Something, anything, which would help me locate their phone number.

I finally found a phone number online. I was terrified my brother would answer. Terrified I'd done something wrong and he'd be angry with me. Terrified of hearing his voice. It took me the better part of a week to get up the courage to call.

When I heard Angie's voice, I was flooded with relief. She asked me if I wanted to talk with my brother, and said he wasn't home. I told her I'd called to talk to her. We talked, she told me about her sisters and brother and children and grand children. I think at some point we both wept. When I asked her how she was doing, I was stunned by her answer.

Angie had to go to work (she was a hospice RN), so I told her I'd call again soon. Tears were streaming down my face when I hung up. Angie was fighting cancer and my Brother was dealing with serious health issues.

For a few months, she and I spoke semi regularly. I learned about her trip to see her sister. I actually spoke with my brother on the phone (nearly fainted when I heard his voice). For a too short time, it felt as there was a chance he and I could be siblings again.

I guess I must have screwed up, don't quite know what happened. I was told I had sent them too many things, was stressing them, they didn't have room. I had a couple of small strokes (no one's fault), and stopped calling for a while. I April I sent my brother some birthday presents.

One day, out of the blue Angie called and told me I was killing her with all the stuff I'd been sending. It was all I could do to hold back the tears. I could barely talk at the time, so I listened and told Angie I was recovering from another stroke and a pulmonary embolism. My memory wasn't the same, my vision was off, my thinking was muddled.

Thinking Angie's outburst was because of something my brother had said, Johnnie send him an email. He then said we were blocking their phone number. "You're making yourself sick trying to figure out why your brother doesn't want to know you. So no more calls. The doctor said no more stress, or you'll never get better." So as of April 2013, I've stopped calling. For now I'm working on regaining my physical health.

Sex Education Class and Mom

When I was in the sixth grade I had to attend a sex education class. As had started school two years earlier than most, at 10 years old, I was the youngest girl there. In many ways I was also the most naive.

After giving us sample Kotex pads and paraphernalia and lots of pamphlets to read, the teacher turned off the lights and started the projector. We watched hours of old movies. The girls wore long poodle skirts with lots and lots of petticoats. They wore ankle socks with black and white saddle shoes. They talked funny and said "gee whiz" a lot. I remember hearing girls from my class giggling in the back of the auditorium.

They told us about a woman's uterus, about menstruation and the changes that happened in a girl's body when she grew up. They told us boys had a penis, and also underwent changes as they grew up.

They said babies were made when sperm from a married man entered his wife's uterus. Then the movie ended and class was over for the day.

All the way home, the big discussion was how sperm got from the man to the woman. Try as we might, no one could figure it out.

"OK, we know they have to be married." said my friend Sally. *"That's a given."*

"My cousin Marion got pregnant BEFORE she was married." Said one of the girls walking with us. *"How do you suppose that happened?"*

"The guy who got her pregnant must have been a married man." Said Sally wisely. *"How else could she have gotten pregnant."*

"I think I know." Said Janet. Everyone went quiet. *"Ever notice the end of a wedding? The part when the priest makes the bride and groom drink out of the same cup?"*

"Yeah, so what?" said one of the girls. *"What's drinking out of a stupid cup have to do with getting knocked up?"* Everyone giggled.

Janet rolled her eyes at the girl. *"Don't you get it, the wife ALWAYS gets pregnant after drinking out of the same cup as her husband."*

Snapshots from a Broken Camera

"Oh my God!" squealed Rita *"I'm pregnant I'm pregnant!"* *"My brother and I drink out of the same cup all the time."*

Giggles turned to laughter. *"Rita you haven't even started having periods, so you can't get pregnant."* Said Sally. *"Besides, you drank out of your BROTHER'S cup. Everyone knows that brothers and sisters can't make babies together. I'm sure I read that somewhere. I mean it's some sort of biological law or rule or something like that."*

That afternoon, when I returned home, I couldn't wait to ask my Mom how sperm got into a woman's uterus. Her response was an angry and instantaneous "Don't ask me that now!"

Curious and not willing to let the subject rest, I continued pestering my Mom for days. Her answer was always the same. "NOT NOW!"

On Friday after Mom picked me up from school, she took me shopping with her at Alpha Beta. In retrospect I should have realized that the grocery store wasn't the best place to be asking about sex. But I was 10 years old, and curious beyond words, so I kept on asking my Mom for an answer.

When we got to the checkout stand my Mom was smiling and talking with the Manager. She always looked happy to see the man. Mom was happy, always a good thing, so I figured now was a time to talk to her again.

I took a deep breath, smiled at my Mom, and quickly blurted out my question. *"Mom, how do sperm get from a husband to his wife?"* The manager was smiling. My Mom coughed loudly and then kicked my leg with her foot.

"My Daughter saw some sex education movies at school this week." said Mom, looking at the Manager with a bored expression. *"She's been pestering me ever since."* The manager broke out laughing. He reached under the counter and pulled out a purple lollipop. *"Here kiddo,"* he said handing me the lollipop, *"I think you may need this."*

When Mom and I exited the store it was pouring outside. The sky was covered with dark grey clouds. I addressed my Mom again. *"How do sperm get from a husband to his wife?"*

Ignoring my question, my Mom reached inside her purse and pulled out her lipstick. She opened the attached mirror and dabbed her lips with color. She put on her white leather driving gloves, then closed her lipstick case and lit up a cigarette.

It was raining and bitterly cold outside, my breath was exiting my body in huge white clouds. Cigarette dangling in her hands, my Mom was staring at me. She paused to flick a piece of tobacco from her lips. *"So you have a question for me."* asked my Mother, almost inaudibly.

Mom took a long draw on her cigarette, paused and then slowly exhaled. *"Do you still want to know?"* she asked again. There was a hard brittle edge to her voice, so I was too scared to answer. *"Do, you, want, to KNOW?"*

Mom's face was shrouded in smoke. I looked at her angry face and felt myself shivering ... more out of fear than from the cold.

"Do, you, want, to KNOW?" Mom exhaled again. *"I guess you must, because you've been asking me the same question for days."* Mom was talking slowly and purposefully.

Mom walked away from Alpha Beta's automatic sliding door, away from prying eyes, and curious people. She leaned against the store's bright tile wall, pulled back her cigarette and held it in her hand. The tip was covered with her lipstick.

Mom glanced slowly up and down the store entrance. When she was sure no one was near, she started talking. *"The man takes his THING ..."* she paused for effect *"pushes it in you ..."* Not looking at me, she continued, pointing to her groin area. She paused again to inhale deeply on her cigarette, *"and pisses!"*

"No Mama, no ..." I gasped.

"Now you know." said Mom in an unhurried and steady voice. *"You asked and now you know. You know what I put up with, and what I endured to have YOU!"* She took one last draw on her cigarette, exhaled, and then tossed it onto cement below her.

Mom was staring at me. *Anymore questions?* The faintest outline of a smile was forming on her lips. *No? That's what I thought.* She stubbed out her cigarette with her shoe. Then, she put on her plastic rain bonnet and strode out to the car. *"Get in"* she ordered, pointing the passenger side of the car. *"I need to get home and fix dinner."*

I sat in the car looking at the rain pouring down onto the windshield. *"She hates my Dad and my Brother."* I thought to myself, while fighting back tears. *"She wants me to hate them to."*

Snapshots from a Broken Camera

Mom's car sputtered to life. The sound of the windshield wipers matched the sound of my beating heart. I was crying silently, tears pouring down my face. I watched through the windshield as the world, my world, melted and blended into the rain.

It was cold outside and even colder inside the car. The windshield was turning white with frost. My Mom had turned to ice, and I feared I would never feel warm again.

My father, my brother, my grandfather, my uncles and friends ... all the boys and men I knew and loved, had been reduced to something dirty, something nasty, something evil and bad. Something to be flushed down a toilet. I wanted to die. Would have rather died than think of them that way. "I love you Papa." I thought to myself " I always will."

I felt my soul melting away with the rain. My soul flowed down the street, into the gutter and out to sea, as far away from my Mother as it could go.

～16 August 2013

For the past week I've been having almost nonstop flashbacks. The last two days have been nightmarish.

Can't sleep, wake up screaming. God, the dreams, the images, the memories, are too much. Can't stop shaking today. Tried eating, my stomach's a mess. I eat and my heart pounds. I eat and I run to the bathroom. So scared, so God damned scared. My heart's pounding.

Was laying on bed trying to watch TV before getting ready to see my neurologist, Dr Spurgeon. My Tourettes are off the chart. Can't sit still. Can't stop shaking. Johnnie heard me screaming. He came in and found me screaming and writhing in bed, feeling like a freak. Scared Johnnie. Scared the dog, who's barking at my screams. Scared the cat. Scaring myself.

"Do you want to go to E.R.?" Asked my husband Johnnie.

Dear God, what on earth for? What would they treat? How would they see me? How would they judge me? Nutcase Jeanne, lock her up and send her to the loony bin. So NO I don't want to go to the fucking emergency room THANK YOU VERY MUCH.

I keep having flashes of fists and hands and arms. They're moving so fast, the images of them are almost too blurred to make out. Relentless, they come at my face and my body. In my head and I hear myself scream and scream and scream.

I'm little and naked and afraid. Someone is hitting me. Someone I can't quite see. I can't make out the face. I can't see if it's a man or a woman. Someone bigger than me. Someone takes me and pulls my legs up and starts fingering my privates. I struggle and fight to push away, more hands slap and punch me, push me down onto something cold and hard.

I feel something push against my back side. Over and over and over again. Now something is pushing against my anus. Suddenly the room tilts on its side. I feel pain. Unyielding relentless searing pain. Over and over and over again. "Mama, Mama!" I scream in terror both in my head and here at home. "Papa, Papa, where are you Papa?" I'm crying in my head, I'm fighting back tears now. My face, my top, damp with tears.

Where is everyone? Why am I alone. I have died. The only part of me alive is pain.

Snapshots from a Broken Camera

I can't stand this. Nobody could. I'm so scared. I don't know where this is coming from. I can't know. Never, it's too much. Too God damned much. There's blood, I see blood. I smell blood. I taste blood mixed with something else. Why doesn't anyone see the blood? Where is my family? Where are my Mom and Dad? Where am I? Doesn't anyone hear me? Will anyone ever hear me? Will anyone ever stop this nightmare?

I can't breathe. I can't breathe. My heart is beating so fast I think it'll explode in my chest. Please don't let me die this way. Please don't let me die alone. Stars Stars, I see Stars. They swirl around my face, millions of tiny sparks. I can't breathe. They sky is turning grey. So many sparks. They sky is turning dark grey. Millions and millions of sparks. I can't breathe. I try to scream, but nothing comes out.

Went to the endocrinologist yesterday. They found some nodules on my thyroid. Sort'a kind'a normal, sort'a kind'a not. Most likely nothing. But I've got a lot of nodules. Some are sort'a kind'a big, too big to ignore. Having a biopsy in a month. Four small pricks in my neck with a 28 gauge needle. Not a big deal. Just one more fucking thing. That's all. Screw it!

My INR, blood clotting level keeps coming back high. Yesterday it was 3.5, last week it was 3.8. Not off the charts high, but still high enough to skip one dose of warfarin last night. Feel out of control. Feel scared. Sometimes I don't know how to keep it together.

This book is too much. Memories keep coming at me. The flashbacks are almost more than I can handle. Took a break from writing yesterday, and just worked on the cover. No new stories, just spell checking and copy editing. I hate this damned book and what it represents. I hate remembering.

I feel sick. I feel scared. I feel out of control.

A small voice inside keeps crying out. "Please don't let them hurt me. I don't want to die this way. Please make it stop." I feel her pushing against my stomach, and moving around in my head. Oh God, how freakishly insane this must all sound.

When I first started integration, first started learning to coexist with all my shared parts, I felt movement in my body and in my head. I heard voices. The doctor had said that was normal, other dissociatives (people with MPD/DID) sometimes feel the same thing.

When I was first diagnosed with MPD my Mom told me not to tell anyone. Mom was visiting me at the psych unit. "You need a vacation. Just go away for a couple of days and you'll be fine." She had said. "Don't ever tell anyone you hear voices." They'll think you're nuts, not a psychic like me. I hear voices and I NEVER tell anyone BUT my clients.

"I didn't anyone I hear voices Mom, trust me."

"So how did the doctor find out miss know it all?"

"Doctor White asked Mama. All she did was ask."

"So now when someone, a doctor, asks if you're hearing voices YOU SAY YES?"

"No Mama, it was nothing like that. I didn't say yes. People, other therapists and nurses noticed changes in me."

"Changes? What in the hell does THAT mean?

"I don't know Mama. I don't Know."

That day one of the psych techs, a friend of mine, took me into a treatment room. "What's this bull shit I hear about you thinking you have MPD?"

"I never said that. I don't know where you're getting that."

"You're full of fucking shit. The doctor wrote down you've been losing time."

"I don't know what you're talking about."

He was standing up against me, his face inches from mine. "You are so full of shit!" He screamed, while pushing me against the wall. "There's no such thing as MPD and YOU fucking know it! It's a God Damned fallacious disease. You just want fucking attention."

My friend, someone I'd known for years, had worked with at various hospitals, was screaming me down in a sound proof treatment room. I didn't know what to do. When he was done screaming at me, and finally left the room, I slid down onto the floor. I sat there crying for I don't know how long. I sat there until one of the charge nurses came to use the room and found me inside still crying.

For the record, I eventually told the director of nursing what had happened between my friend and I. I DID NOT file an official complaint, as I didn't want my friend to lose his job. I also wanted her to get the word out to the psych staff that I didn't believe I had MPD. The idea Dr White thought I might be suffering from it terrified me.

It would be two years before I was even able to admit I was losing time and needed treatment. The process of integration was hard and took years to complete. But then that's another story for another time.

Snapshots from a Broken Camera

I haven't had dissociative episodes in over a decade. Not until recently. Now I'm dealing with recovery from a six pack of mini strokes and a pulmonary embolism. Toss in possible thyroid cancer, and my emotions are a tad over the top. Like they say in the medical books "I'm coo coo for cocoa puffs".

Forgot to take my Lorazepam last night. The alarm woke me up to take it, but I guess I fell back to sleep. I thought I remembered opening the box and tipping it into my mouth and the drinking some water. But 0.5mg Lorazepam tablets are small, about the size of saccharine tablets. When I put my pill box away, the night tablet was still inside.

I want to go home! I want to feel safe. I wish to God I had family around me. No offense Johnnie. Johnnie tries to care, but he's fragile himself and easily overwhelmed. He rarely sees me this way. To be fair NOBODY sees me this way. I don't usually loose it this big unless I'm all by myself.

I guess that's part of the reason that feeling this out of control scares me. Because I NEVER lose control in this big a way, even at the worst of times. Fact is, there are only about three people who've ever seen me CLOSE to this bad, and one of them is dead. The young part inside me, the one missing family, is terrified beyond words. Inconsolable. The memories and the pain she feels is beyond description.

She hears my thoughts, hears conversations with my doctors, knows I've been sick, knows I take medications. When my head hurts she fears I'm having another stroke. "Like Opa had and eventually killed him. Like Mama had." When my heart beats too fast she fears I'm having a heart attack. "Like Amy had and killed her. Like Uncle Walt had and killed him. Like Dad Had and killed him."

The thyroid thing has put her over the edge. (Me too a little) Memories of being choked, strangled, stuck with needles, force medicated and worse. Memories of unspeakably cruel events. Memories of pain.

It's quarter to 9 and I have to stop. My appointment with Dr Spurgeon is at 9:30 so I need to dress quickly. Hopefully the Lorazepam and beta blocker will have kicked in by the time I arrive. Don't want to show up acting like Linda Blair in The Exorcist. I can see it now. "Hiya Doc, hang on for a sec while I tap dance on the ceiling for ya."

God I wish I were normal. Geeze, I'd be happy just knowing what in the hell normal looked like. It sure as hell isn't me. Let's hear it for mental illness, the gift that keeps on giving!

Wouter Kabouter

"We are not only our brother's keeper;
in countless large and small ways, we are our brother's maker."
  Bonaro Overstreet, American poet and psychologist

I loved my Uncle Walt. Long before I learned he was really my half brother, I loved him. Long before alcohol had stolen his health, and blunted his mind. I loved him.

I knew him as a sweet natured man, with a kind heart and a caring soul. Walt's birth certificate says he was born in 1937. His death certificate says he was born in 1940. Either way he was around eighteen when I was born. I was three when he married.

I remember his beautiful wife Sharon. I remember the birth of their children. First Daughter Suzette Michelle, born 1960 ... whom I knew as "Michelle" ... sweet natured beautiful soul. She looked like a perfect porcelain doll. Then came Wouter Jr., and Edward, Shanna, Desiree, Denise.

Sharon had 12 children in all, forgive me for not knowing everyone's names. We haven't stayed in touch. I'm not great at staying in touch. Too much time spent taking care of Mom. Too much time spent taking care of Dad. Too much time taking care of too many others.

Walt moved in to my parent's home a few years before his death. He was drinking full time then. His liver was gone. So much damage, so much heartache, so much sorrow.

Walt talked about his children constantly. He loved and missed them so. He talked about all he had accomplished in life. Everything lost to the ravages of time and too much alcohol.

I was still working then, as a respiratory therapist. I tried to help Walt stop drinking. I took him to AA meetings. When Walt had chest pains, I took him to the E.R., to be checked out where I worked. I paid for his care.

When I found him passed out in the street outside our home, I picked him up and took him for food. It didn't take much to get him drunk. Alcohol was breaking down, had broken down, his body. His liver was shot ... cirrhosis. The muscles of his heart were slowly shutting down ... cardiomyopathy. His teeth were literally rotting in his mouth.

I tried to hide Walt's continued alcohol use from my Mom. She believed he was sober. She believed his body would heal. She believed her love could save him.

Snapshots from a Broken Camera

"Wouter Kabouter", she would call him. Speaking to him as if he were still an infant. Walt would come lay next to my Mom on the bed. She would comb his hair and tell him stories about the infant Wouter she had loved and cared for. Stories about the Netherlands, the house they lived in and how he grew up.

"You left me." he said accusingly. You left me when I was seven!"

"I got married Wouter." she whispered "The war was over. Everything was new for you. You had school then, and Mama and Papa. You had everyone."

"I didn't have you Nel."

Mom teared up. "Wouter Kabouter" she sighed "You still had me, and you were always in my heart."

I didn't know how to react to their conversations. I felt uncomfortable hearing my Mom speaking to Walt using baby talk. My Uncle Martin had told me "there's no way in hell I'd let her talk to me that way."

One afternoon I came home from work and found Walt laying face down in the gutter. He was sandwiched between his car and the curb, an empty wine bottle in his hand. It took me a while to rouse him, let alone get him up from the ground.

I dragged him over to my car. "What have you eaten today?" He just looked at me and shrugged. His hands were shaking as he struggled to light a cigarette.

I took Walt to La Fonda's in Santa Ana. Close to his AA meeting. I sat with him while he forced down some food. Mostly I listened to him talk about how much he missed his children, and how much he wanted to stop drinking so he could get back into their lives.

Out of the blue Walt told me he wanted to sleep with me. I asked him if he was out of his fucking mind. He told me he didn't want to do anything to me. That "he couldn't get it up", so even if he wanted to do something he couldn't.

Then he said he was attracted to me, had been attracted to me for a long time. "I like women built like you." My brain short circuited. "I want to hold you, and have you hold me."

While trying to wrap my brain around what Walt was saying to me, he threatened to kill me. "If you tell your mother, tell ANYONE, what I just said to you ... I'll kill you."

"You don't have the balls." I answered

"I'll kill you if you tell your Mother."

I reached over and grabbed a knife from the table next to us. "Whatever you say Walt. But NOBODY tells me what I can or cannot say, or to whom. So I guess you'll just have to kill me." I handed him the knife.

Walt looked at me with a strange expression. " You think I'm kidding. But I will kill you if you tell ANYONE!"

"You don't have the balls." I said, placing the blade of the knife (still in his hand) against my chest. I'll even give you the first cut. After that I'll break your fucking fingers."

Walt dropped the knife on the table. "Jesus you're a scary bitch."

"You got that right. You don't know the half of it Walt." Then I took him to his A.A. meeting.

When I got back home, I told my Mom that Walt had said he wanted to sleep with me. True to form, Mom didn't believe a word I said. She told me Walt would never say anything like that to me, his niece. Not HER Walt. She told me I was a horrible person for even imagining such a thing from her Wouter Kabouter. I was insane.

"You dreamed it." Three words I'd heard hundreds of times before. Mom told me I dreamt it when Steve first molested me ... when Steve ran over my foot with his car ... after I was raped ... WHENEVER she didn't want to hear or face what I'd said. "You dreamed it." My three least favorite words in the English language.

A few days later my Mom waved me into her bedroom. "Jeannika, stay away from Walt" She whispered.

"Mom, what on earth are you talking about?"

"He, Walt, told me he wants to sleep with me. Did you hear me Jeannika? Walt wants to have sex with me. Be careful he might hurt you."

"What did you just say Mom?"

"Don't make me repeat it. You heard me."

"But Mom, Walt would NEVER say anything like that! He's your brother. A Brother would NEVER ask his older Sister to sleep with them. So You must be mistaken. You must have dreamed it Mom." Mom was crying when I left the her bedroom.

Snapshots from a Broken Camera

It's difficult to understand why my Mom was crying when I left her room. She looked so hurt and wounded when I left. I keep wondering if her response was just an act, or if she really didn't remember she'd told me almost the same thing two days prior.

About a month later, while I was getting ready for work, my Mom told me Walt had been having "bad" chest pains for about three hours.

"Why didn't you wake me Mom?"

"Because you need your sleep. I told Walt to take a nice long shower."

"Why would you tell a man with chest pains to take a shower?"

"To make him feel better."

I groaned inwardly and picked up the phone. I didn't want to chance Walt going into cardiac arrest while I drove him to the hospital. So I called 911 and asked them to stop by, just in case, so they could transfer him to E.R. I told them he was conscious, but had been having chest pains for at least three hours. I also gave them his medical history.

The moment I put down the phone, I heard Walt scream "oh shit!" I stepped into his room and found him clutching his chest. A second later he fell onto the bed. I felt for a pulse, he had none. I screamed at my Mom to call 911, but she was in the bathroom being sick.

I called 911, while pulling Walt down onto the floor so I could start CPR. I remember saying "I just called, come right away, my uncle's in full arrest." My Mom grabbed the phone while I started CPR. I was thinking about what Walt would say to me after I revived him.

I felt for a pulse, there was none. Walt's color was grey blue. I breathed five times into Walt's lungs then started compressions again. I noticed he was barrel chested from emphysema and his ribs were brittle as hell. Each time I pushed down on his chest I felt ribs cracking beneath my hands. I kept apologizing as I continued compressions.

20 compressions, 2 breaths, 20 compressions, 2 breaths, check for pulse. Over and over and over again I continued, all the while waiting for Walt to return. I was shocked when he didn't. The paramedics arrived, the same team I worked with at Santa Ana Tustin Community.

The paramedics hooked Walt up to a monitor, then told me to hold compressions for a second. Walt's heart was in an aginal rhythm. An aginal rhythm isn't a good sign. It's what you see when ventricular fibrillation ends and death begins.

One of the paramedics intubated Walt and was now using an ambu bag to resuscitate him with oxygen. I continued doing compressions. One of the paramedics who knew me from work, came into the room and asked me what I was doing there. "I live here." was my breathless answer.

He asked one of the other paramedics to relieve me. "On the count of three" I pressed down once, twice, three times and then pulled back. "Someone check the monitor." Someone called out in the room. I sat still, staring at the monitor, hoping and against hope Walt would come back with a better heart rhythm. "Still aginal."

I got up and ran into the restroom. My heart was pounding, I felt dizzy and sick to my stomach. All I could think of was his children, and how I'd let everyone down.

The paramedics transferred Walt to the nearest hospital, where he was pronounced dead 30 minutes later.

A few days after Walt's funeral I returned to work. My supervisor put me on code call, which was normally light duty. Normally not that many people go into cardiac arrest on any given shift. That night there were two traumas and four or five codes. All told I did CPR on 7 people, all of whom died. Normally that wouldn't have been a problem. Normally I'd have gone on from one patient to the next without breaking down.

I remember the very first code I worked on. I remember climbing on top of a bed and doing CPR for the first time. The first person I saw die. I thought I was going to die myself. More than anything else in the world I wanted to stop CPR, run screaming out of that room and never return.

I wanted to be an artist ... a musician ... to live my life creating beautiful things and thinking beautiful thoughts. Instead I remolded myself in my Mom's image. To make her proud. So she would love me, and I could feel worthy of God's grace.

So I stayed and pushed on a stranger's chest as he lay dying. Eventually I learned to pull a part of myself back, to disconnect from the fear and sadness of it all. Eventually I became good at doing what had to be done when people were sick or dying. Living life on automatic pilot, while not thinking about much else. After Walt died I was no longer able to disconnect.

That first night back at work, when they gave me code call and seven people died, I lost it. I felt the weight of all the family members who had loved and cared for these dying people. Then during lunch, I locked myself in the 7th floor nurses station and wept for them all.

Snapshots from a Broken Camera

Two weeks later, while driving home from the store, a car careened through a red light. It barely missed my car. My heart didn't skip a beat. I didn't start shaking. I didn't feel anything at all. I remember thinking "damn, too bad he missed." It was then I realized that I wished I were dead.

I went home and called the psych unit at the hospital I worked at. I explained what had just happened, and that I thought I was suicidal. They set up and appointment for me to speak with a psych nurse.

I didn't cry after Walt died. I didn't cry at his funeral. Riddled with guilt over the death of my uncle, I was crying now. After speaking with the psych nurse I signed myself in for treatment. I cried for days during my first psychiatric hospitalization. The first of many.

When I got out of the hospital I moved out of my parent's home. I couldn't stand seeing where Walt had died while under my care. My life was out of control. The guilt I felt wouldn't leave. I began planning my suicide.

I wrote letters to everyone I loved. Made out checks to people. Then mailed everything out. I taped a letter on the front door telling my roommate NOT to go in the living room. I put towels on the floor, got a huge plastic bag and lined it with a towel. Then I took my roommate's new 22 rifle and put 6 bullets in it.

I lay down on the floor and placed my upper body inside the plastic bag. I put the rifle barrel in my mouth and pulled the trigger. I remember hearing a police helicopter flying over head and thinking it's true that hearing is the last thing to go. I felt peaceful and grateful there was no pain.

I remember thinking if I'd known suicide was going to be such a wonderful experience I would have killed myself long ago. After a few minutes, when I noticed I was still breathing, I realized the rifle had failed to go off. So I took a deep breath and pulled the trigger again. Nothing.

Now I was really scared. I'd grown up around guns and rifles. I'd fired guns and rifles. Why hadn't the rifle gone off? More importantly why wasn't I dead? Shaken and scared half out of my mind, I picked up the rifle, wrapped it in a towel and ran outside to my car. I opened the trunk and quickly locked the rifle inside.

I called the suicide hotline and said I'd just tried to kill myself. "Guess you just didn't try hard enough." said a disinterested voice on the other end of the line. "Excuse me?" I said, surprised. "You heard me honey. You're obviously full of shit." Shaken, I hung up.

I called my psychiatrist and told him what had just happened. He asked me if I was able to drive myself back to the hospital. I said yes, and was admitted that night.

While I was hospitalized my roommate cashed the check I sent him with my suicide note, and used my name to apply for a bunch of credit cards. He then charged hundreds of dollars in my name, which I was eventually forced to repay.

I eventually moved back in with my parents. Went on state disability and quit my job as a respiratory therapist. I returned to school to study computer programming and desk top publishing.

Years later I was diagnosed as having Multiple Personality Disorder, and started the long process of integration. Most importantly, I began repairing my soul. The first step was forgiving myself for not having been able to save Walt. The second was allowing myself to remember the past.

I have never forgotten Walt or his family. It no longer matters if he was my uncle or my brother. I loved him, and that's all that matters. I know now the lies we endured, damaged us both. I'm sorry Walt lost his life. I'm sorry I didn't have the skills to save him.

My Trip Through Inner Space

On August 5, 1967, Disneyland unveiled a ride called "Adventure Through Inner Space". I remember at the time it was heralded as groundbreaking. It propelled people around on Disney's brand new Omnimover system.

The idea behind Omnimover was to place riders inside a sort'a kind'a live action movie. You were pushed and pulled and spun from one action scene to another. Sound followed with you, from within your seat. Lights changed around you, as action segments changed from one to the next.

> *Sometimes it feels (to me at least) as if my life has been like a never ending ride on an Omnimover system. I can't get off, and every time I think my life has settled down there's another twist to deal with.*

So many people, so many relationships, so much chaos. No way to get off. The only exit, it would seem, is death.

I used to keep a list of all the men I had relationships with. I thought of it as my own personal "Walk of Shame". The hard cold truth is, in my entire life I have NEVER had a normal relationship with a normal man. To a one, every man I have ever been with ... every man I have ever loved ... has been seriously flawed.

I don't know if that says more about me, or if it is simply in people's nature to be flawed. I only know I've never been with a man who wasn't lugging around a great deal of personal luggage. Which I probably could have handled, if it wasn't for the fact I often ended up with that luggage smacking me in the face.

I married Michael (my first husband) so I could get the hell out of Dodge. My Mom, God love her, was "coo-coo for cocoa puffs" (should be a real medical term) and was quickly turning me into the same.

I could spend my entire life writing about the things Mom did to me, (did to others) and never express the full horror of it all. Basically Mom was nuts. Mom was a bottomless pit of need. Unfortunately, Mom's brain wasn't equipped with an OFF button. She was unrelenting, which meant the damage she caused was inexorable and irreversible. For those of us in her headlights, there was no exit and no escape from the pain.

My Mom molested me, although she would have argued the fact. I don't think she believed the things she did to my private parts constituted molestation, although they most certainly did. She believed, or so she said, that she was a good mother.

My Mom used to hit me, although she would have argued the fact. I don't think she believed that slapping or shaking could cause the same kind of damage as punching, although they most certainly did. After all, she was so much better about things than her Mom had been to her. She never beat me with fists or sticks or worse.

My Mom tortured me, although she would have argued the fact. I don't think she believed the things she said or did constituted torture, although they most certainly did. She believed she was teaching me useful life lessons.

My Mom tried to kill me, MANY TIMES, although she would have argued the fact. I don't think she believed the things she said or did could have caused harm, let alone kill me, although they most certainly did.

Boundaries were never Mom's thing. Lines were blurred between the two of us. She believed we were one entity. She believed she owned me.

> *Mom believed the closeness she and I shared entitled her to do and say ANYTHING she wanted to me and my friends and my boyfriends and my classmates and anyone else I might have known. She believed she ALWAYS knew best. She believed she was a good and kind person. She believed she didn't hurt people. She was wrong ... on ALL counts.*

Mom loved pulling chest hair off of men. Mom loved pulling chest hair off my boyfriends. Mom loved pulling the chest hair off my Brother and his male friends. If they protested, she'd call them silly and laugh. If they cried out in pain, she'd call them babies and laugh. If they fought back she would fly into a rage. If they slapped her, she'd slap back HARDER.

There was no way in hell that any NORMAL boy or man would put up with that kind of bullshit. So my brother and his friends didn't hang around the house much. There was no way in hell that any NORMAL boy would want to have a relationship with me AND MY MOTHER. So I didn't have many boyfriends.

I married Michael to get the hell out of Dodge. Not because I wanted to. He and I had simply wanted to live together. Only Mom was worried. Not about me. She was worried about what the neighbors would think ... worried about what her friends would think ... worried about what our minister would think. So we got married.

Snapshots from a Broken Camera

Mom hated **EVERY** man I ever had a relationship with, **EVERY** man I dated, **EVERY** man I ever married. She would describe their **EVERY** flaw to me ... and anyone else willing to listen ... for hours on end. She would dissect their **EVERY** imperfection with surgical precision. Then when the relationship failed, as they were bound to do, she would remind you how correct her perceptions had been. Losers, losers all. "Men are pigs Darling, it's not your fault."

Mom hated **EVERY** woman my brother ever had a relationship with, **EVERY** woman he dated, **EVERY** woman he ever married. She would describe their **EVERY** flaw to him ... and anyone else willing to listen ... for hours on end. She would dissect their every imperfection with surgical precision. Then when the relationship failed, as they were bound to do, she would remind him how correct her perceptions had been. Losers, losers all. "Woman are pigs Darling, it's not your fault."

That either of us ever managed to maintain long term relationships with ANYONE is astounding. Funny thing is, in all my life, I have never been able to tell when someone liked me. I so disliked myself. I so hated my body. I felt so worthless. I always assumed no man would ever like me, let alone find me attractive. When one did, I wondered about HIS mental health.

I have few pictures of the men I have loved ... because after it was over, Mom ALWAYS tore them up FOR ME. I have no connections with many people from my past ... because Mom made it impossible for me to do so.

Michael

I met Michael while we were both in high school. He was in my adaptive P.E. class. A class I was assigned to after my car accident. Michael was silly and funny and sensitive. He'd play shark in the pool and attack people's feet from below. If you were having a bad day, he'd either tell you a joke or give you a hug. People liked Michael and he liked them.

He ran the stage lights for drama. One afternoon, when he was setting up and testing the lights he pulled me inside. He had a bar stool setup on stage. There was a mike next to it.

"Bring your guitar and sing." he said "pointing to the stool." I need to test the lights and sound." It was after 3pm, and no one was there. Other than Michael and I, the room was empty. I took out my guitar and played and sang for what felt like hours. The lights blinding me from anything beyond three feet of me. After 20 minutes or so, I slid off the seat and over to the microphone. I told Michael I my voice was tired. I was done.

Suddenly the room was filled with applause. Michael turned the lights up and I saw the room was now filled with people. I was so terrified that I dropped my guitar. Michael looked at me and smiled. He took away the mike. "Can this girl sing or what?"

I wanted to live with Michael. Pure and simple, no complications. Mom forced "her" complications on me and on Michael. We were both painfully young in those days. Marriage wasn't in the best interest for either of us, but she didn't care.

Michael was always freer than I, bolder and less afraid. He embodied the 70's sexual revolution lifestyle. The whole revolution thing scared the shit out of me.

He brought people home. He encouraged me to bring people home. He encouraged me to participate in sex with multiple partners. I don't know if he realized it, but I was terrified.

> *There was a time in my life when I would sleep with almost ANYONE who showed an interest. Not for the sex. Lord God almighty, not for the sex. More than anything else in the world, I simply wanted to feel loved. I simply wanted to be held. I simply wanted to feel special.*

> *Funny thing about sleeping around. In the end, it NEVER made me feel special or loved. Sleeping around made me feel sad lonely and unlovable. Sleeping around made me feel like a worthless whore.*

One day Michael invited the wife of a man we'd been having a sexual relationship with, to join us in a four way. While I had learned to be around naked men, I was terrified of seeing a woman naked. Terrified of laying next to a naked woman. Terrified out of my mind.

I remember hearing the man tell me "You know you want it", while inviting me join him on my waterbed. I felt as if I were in a trance. I kept hearing his words echoing inside my head over and over and over again.

> *"You know you want it ... you know you want it ... you know you want it"*

No longer in my body, no longer in the room. I watched my body climb into my bed and straddle the man, who was laying on his back. " You know you want it" He said, sliding his erect penis beneath me. My heart was thudding in my ears, as he pushed himself deep inside me. The instant he entered I climaxed. The instant I climaxed I wanted to die.

My ears were ringing loudly. But I could still hear the man's voice, taunting me. Michael was next to me on the bed laughing. The room was spinning and I felt like vomiting.

Snapshots from a Broken Camera

The man was smiling "I knew I could make you cum." I was shaking, filled with fear, horror and shame. Mistaking my trembling for passion, the man continued grinding himself inside me. "I knew I could make you cum, and I'm going to make you cum again." I couldn't move. I could barely breath. Trembling and rigid with fear, I wanted to run away. I wanted to die.

When the man finally climaxed I quickly slid off the bed. I ran into my bathroom and vomited. I think I cleaned myself up. I kept hearing the man's voice repeating inside my head. You know you want it ... you know you want it ... you know you want it"

I heard a familiar woman's voice whispering in my ear. "Whore."

I remember returning to my bedroom. Michael and the man were making love to the other woman. She was making love to them. The sound of their lovemaking and the sloshing of the waterbed burned my ears. I was near hysteria. They were talking to me, Michael and the man. I heard some say I was acting selfish. The last thing I remember is running.

The woman's voice returned. "Whore, filthy whore. Stay naked, like the whore you are."

I fled from the voice. I fled from the room.
I fled from my body.

I remember running for miles down a dark sidewalk lined with thousands of black trees. Every once in a while I heard the man's voice in the distance. "You know you want it ... you know you want it ... you know you want it" So I ran harder and harder until I was breathless and the trees and the sky and the cement had all turned black ... and I had ceased to be.

It would be decades before I learned fear can trigger orgasms. Years and years more, before I was finally able to think of myself as something more than a filthy whore. Years when I felt worthless and dead inside.

To this day I can barely remember the men I had sex with while married to Michael. Nor can I remember sex with the men who came after our divorce.

I can't imagine what having a normal sex life would be like, or if it would even be possible for me to experience one. Truth be told, having sex has is on the bottom of my to do list.

I learned my youngest alter, the one who endured the worst abuse, comes out after I climax. I can't imagine the fear she must feel. Nor can I imagine how men I have been with have felt if I began crying after climax. That said, if I never had sex again I'd be just fine.

I left Michael for many reasons. He hit me. He had affairs. He lied. He stole things. He belittled me. He talked me into a sexual lifestyle I never wanted. I used to tell myself I was lucky to get away. Almost everyone I spoke with agreed. Yet I still miss his friendship, his exuberance, his energy, and his way of looking adversity in the eye and saying "Fuck You".

Steve

I met Steve in high school. I'd seen him around campus struggling to carry his books. He had broken his leg and was on crutches. I walked up to him and asked him if he needed some help. We became friends.

Steve is a few years old than I. Back then we were both so young. He and his brothers would come to my home. Sometimes just to hang out and talk about life. Other times to sleep over when his Mom was away for the weekend.

His Mother became one of my Mom's friends. Steve and his brothers became my brothers and best friends. The memory I have of Steve kneeling down to say his prayers will forever be etched upon my soul.

I don't know when friendship changed into something more. We dated like teenagers do. Movies, amusement parks, walks. He was the first boy to kiss me. The first boy to hold my hand. The first boy to treat me like I was special. Eventually we fought over something (I can't remember what) and went back to being just friends.

Steve was there when I married Michael. He was there again when I left him. After my divorce, while he was recovering from a motorcycle accident, we reconnected. He asked me to marry him and I said yes. He was a friend and someone I always thought I'd be safe with.

I left Steve because he hated my Mom. He forced me to choose, when I could not. Friends since childhood, I watched him grow from a boy into a man. This super smart man/boy, who loved me for who I was . Almost everyone I spoke with said I was well rid of him.

Ralph

I met Ralph while working at Good Samaritan Hospital. I was slender then and all sorts of guys were asking me out, most of them scared me.

Snapshots from a Broken Camera

Ralph spent his lunch hour sitting and reading in the cafeteria. I have always loved books, so one day I asked what he was reading. Eventually we became friends. Eventually friendship turned to love.

I felt safe with Ralph. I felt loved by Ralph. I felt free with Ralph. For an all too brief time I had it all. But things were changing. I was a borderline anorexic. Five days a week I lived on Liquid Sego and Doritos. One day a week I'd eat normally. One day a week I'd fast. It was how I controlled my feelings, my life, and my weight.

Gradually I began fasting more and more. Over time I went from 5 cans of Sego a day to 1. Sometimes I'd overeat and then puke everything up. I didn't do it on purpose. The thought of eating so much disgusted me, and food just came up on its own. Eventually vomiting became second nature to me. Eventually vomiting made me sick.

I came down with herpes ... a bunch of us at the hospital did. I went to a doctor who treated my herpes with massive steroid injections (which make herpes worse) and charged me lots of money. He said he would cure me. He nearly killed me. I had no idea.

One day, after months of massive steroid injections, the doctor closed down his office. No referrals, no advice, nada. A few weeks later I came home from work, sat down on my bed and fell over onto the floor. I couldn't get up. My health slid downhill from there. I kept getting sick, running fevers and could barely move.

I'm not sure when, but Ralph had started drinking again. It was a hard time for both of us.

In the end I left Ralph because he had an alcohol problem. The AA councilor I spoke with said it was what would be best for both of us. I used to tell myself I was helping Ralph face his problems. Almost everyone I spoke with agreed. Still I left the love of my life, and the person who knew me best. A man who loved me in spite of my past. A man I still miss.

S.F.E.

I met S.F.E. via "BBW" Big Beautiful Woman magazine. I Met a lot of people that way. I was fat, and the people I wrote to in BBW, didn't care. S.F.E., was about 20 years older than me. He was an underwriter at Union Bank. He was educated and snooty and constantly put me down. I felt worthless and accepted his put downs as a sign he cared.

Actually I owe S.F.E. a huge debt. His constant put downs are what finally gave me the courage to get educated. I learned to write, studied journalism, got published. Learned how to dress, how to wear makeup and learned to how to stand up for myself.

I remember we lived together in a wonderful old apartment I'd gotten near Hollywood and Vine. I loved that place. I heard Marilyn Monroe had lived there before she was famous.

The apartments were old and run down, but the people living there were so vibrant and alive I loved them all. We had a guy who raised pit bulls in his apartment. He had a love hate relationship with his mother. We nick named him "Idiot" for various reasons.

One Sunday Idiot thought it would be a good idea to throw his Mom off the second floor balcony. Luckily there was a pool below. Luckily he didn't miss. Mama was shouting all the way to the pool. She was still shouting when the police came and carted idiot away to jail.

Our apartment was on the first floor. Actually only half of it was on the first floor, the rest was perched above a bunch of parking spaces. Too few parking spaces for all the residents, so I was forced to park on the street.

Every night around 1:30am I'd hear Idiot starting up his car. Besides having major issues with his mother, Idiot had a drinking problem. Which is why every evening, just before the bars closed down and stores stopped selling alcohol, he left to purchase his daily booze.

Unfortunately his parking space was directly below my bedroom. That damned car of his sounded like a tank. EVERY time he'd start up that piece of shit of his, my room was submerged in clouds of toxic gas. Didn't matter if I closed all the windows, the smell still made its way into the apartment.

One evening S.F.E. and I were grocery shopping. I picked up a cucumber, and told S.F.E. that a cucumber would be the perfect thing to shove up the tailpipe of Idiot's car. When S.F.E. looked at me as if I'd suddenly gone off my nut. I explained how cars with blocked tailpipes can't start. And cars that can't start, don't usually make loud noises.

"Would a potato work?" asked S.F.E. "I mean they're fatter than that cucumber."

"Well, yeah they work ... for a little while ... but potatoes shrink fast. Now a cucumber is built to last." We both broke out laughing.

That night, when I went to bed, I'd forgotten about my conversation about clogged tailpipes. So I was surprised when S.F.E. asked me if I had a "LONG" screwdriver he could borrow. He was standing next to my bed with a hammer and particularly large cucumber.

Snapshots from a Broken Camera

"What are you doing to do?" I asked, eyeing the huge cucumber in his hand. "Don't ask" he said. "You're not going to do anything rash are you?". "The tailpipe on Idiot's car is full of holes, so I need to push this thing in as deep as I can."

"Do what you feel you must, but leave me the hell out of it." S.F.E. ended up using a ruler.

At 1:30am S.F.E. woke me up to see if the cucumber would do the job. I could hear Idiot below talking to himself as he got into his car. A moment later I heard the engine trying to turn over. It made a weak whining sound, followed by a single click. Idiot was cursing now. After fifteen minutes he finally gave up trying to start his car and walked to the store.

For two weeks Idiot tried to start his car. For two weeks he had friends over to put in new spark plugs, change the oil and fix a thousand different things which had needed fixing for decades. Still the car wouldn't turn over. That was one hell of a cucumber.

On the third week, I had walked down to the dumpster to throw out some trash. Idiot was standing next to his car, while a group of friends were working on it again. "Try it now." Said one of the friends. Suddenly I heard a massive explosion and watched as the cucumber launched itself from deep within the car's tailpipe.

The cucumber flew a good thirty feet into the air, ending up embedded in a chain link fence from the junkyard next door. Barely missing the junkyard's three legged guard dog, who yelped once, and then quickly took off for parts unknown. The car was purring like a kitten. Luckily Idiot never learned about the cucumber. His car never woke me up again.

I left S.F.E. because he was only using me for my money. He had been born to wealth and privilege, but was now poor. He belittled me for having grown up poor, for being good with money, for being common. Yet he stole my Money, used my credit cards and used me to pay for things he couldn't afford.

He asked me to marry him and gave me a huge "expensive" ring. When I had it appraised I learned it was a cheap CZ set in gold plate. Then he kicked me out so he could take up with a woman who had more to offer. After his new fiancé "drove him crazy" he asked me back. I said no. Almost everyone I spoke with said I'd done the right thing.

After my uncle died, I returned to live with S.F.E. as a roommate ONLY. Because I needed a place to stay and he needed a way to afford his apartment. Eventually, after attempting suicide, I returned to my parent's home.

In the end I left them ALL. I have either run from, or pushed away, Every man I've loved or cared for or felt loved by. I always have. Mostly because sex scares me and I don't know to resolve that issue. Perhaps I never will.

For now I stay with Johnnie, who has become my charge and my friend, (no longer my husband or lover). Legally we are married. But we are both broken. Broken in different ways, but broken nonetheless. We try, as best we can, to care for each other.

Some days, when Johnnie's manic and raging against the world, I hide. Most days I take things one moment at a time. On good days I howl with our dogs. On bad days I meditate, write, play music and pray for grace. Suicide is never far from my mind.

At age 58, I'm just getting to know my youngest alter, the one who endured years of sexual abuse. I don't want to hurt her. I don't want to hurt myself.

I need to be whole, connected to ALL my parts, before I even consider having relations with a man ... ANY man. I need to remember EVERYTHING so I can finally let it all go. I guess that's what so difficult about writing this book. Part of me doesn't want to remember.

Johnnie and I at the Kaanapali Hilton Luau in 2003

ᴥOur Father who art in Heaven

When I was little, I used to wake up at night nauseous, with my heart pounding. I didn't know what was wrong. Didn't know what to do. More often than not I'd wake up my Mom.

"Mama, I don't feel good."

Mom would take me back to my bedroom and make me recite the Lord's prayer over and over and over again. Afterwards, if I was still shaking, Mom would grab her bible, her bottle of valium and go to the kitchen to make fresh tea.

She gave me a cup of tea laced with sugar, and fed me one of her pills. Then she'd open her bible at random and start to read "God's healing message to me". An hour later, we'd recite the Lord's prayer again and she'd put me to bed. She told me God had just healed me and I would be fine in the morning.

I didn't learn I was hypoglycemic (like my Dad) until I was in my 20s. By then my Mom had been force feeding me various types of tranquilizers for most of my life.

When I woke up from a nightmare, or saw someone peering into my bedroom window, it was always the same. Mom said her immortal words "You dreamed it", nothing I ever saw or felt was real.

When I was molested, raped, beaten up or worse it was always the same. "You dreamed it", my three least favorite words in the English language.

The whole Tooth

When I went to the dentist for the first time my Mom didn't come in with me. She didn't see me strapped down in the chair. Didn't see the dentist calling me names. Didn't see the dentist telling me I had a filthy mouth. Didn't see the dentist using his water hose to squirt at my mouth from across the room.

The dentist had said it was a game. He wanted to see if I could sit still enough so the water wouldn't spill out of my mouth. I was too terrified to move. I passed his test.

My Mom liked this dentist, he was handsome and his office was next door to her doctor. She told me that he was the doctor who had pulled out all her teeth. Mom said she told him to pull them, because it was cheaper to wear dentures than pay for yearly dental work.

She said he put her asleep when he pulled her teeth. I heard Mom telling her best friend that the dentist had been fondling her boobs when she woke up. She said the dentist had told her she had an anesthesia induced dream. She believed him.

So she kept going to the handsome dentist. He became our family dentist. He scared me half to death. Whenever he gave me injections I got sick or threw up. For years I always got sick after injections. I was in my 40s when I learned my body can't handle epinephrine.

The dentist told my Mom my brother and I had to come in every six months. Mom said that was too often and not necessary. So she took us in once a year.

The dentist told us get a new tooth brush every month, and NEVER use a tooth brush more than three months. Mon said that was an idiotic idea. Mom said toothbrushes were expensive (five cents back then), too expensive to throw away. EVERYONE knew you used a tooth brush until the bristles were bent flat. Just like she did.

The dentist taught me how to floss and told my Mom my brother and I needed to brush and floss after every meal. Mom said brushing once in the morning was fine. Mom said dental floss was useless and too expensive. Dental floss damaged your gums and your teeth.

Mom didn't believe in dental hygienists or having your teeth cleaned. She said if you got your teeth cleaned the dentist would poke holes in your teeth and create cavities.

If I dropped my tooth brush on the bathroom floor, Mom would rinse it in the sink. When I dropped the tooth brush in the toilet, she soaked it in some bleach. The bottom line was tooth brushes were too expensive to waste.

When I got strep throat, over and over and over again, Mom said God was punishing me. When everyone in my family came down with Strep, the health department came to our home to check conditions. They told my Mom our toothbrushes were too old, and that she had to use hot water and more soap to clean our dishes.

Mom agreed and then continued washing the way she normally did. No new toothbrushes.

When everyone got strep throat again, my Mom said it wasn't her fault. Nothing was ever her fault. So we were all forced to go to the health department for penicillin shots.

I got strep infections so often that penicillin injections were a twice a year thing. When I came down with tonsillitis, and the doctor suggested they come out, Mom said no. I was given a shot and later my Mom told me to pray for God to heal me.

Snapshots from a Broken Camera

When I was in my 20s I nearly died from tonsillitis. I was married then, and my doctor said my tonsils had to come out or I would die. Mom visited me in the hospital and told me the reason I had tonsillitis was because I was having oral sex.

When I told her I hadn't been having oral sex, she said God was punishing me for using the "F" word. She said if I prayed for God's forgiveness I would be healed on the spot. Not trusting God or my Mother, I opted for the tonsillectomy.

Keeping Things Simple

Childhood diseases are a part of life, or at least that's what I've been told. That said, my Brother is seven years older than I am. Whenever HE came down with a childhood disease such as measles or mumps, my Mom would tell me to go play with him.

She said being a Mother was hard work. She said she was too busy to waste time treating my Brother and I separately for diseases we would both eventually come down with. She also believed the earlier you had these diseases, the healthier you'd be in later life. So when children we knew were sick with something my brother had already gotten, I'd be sent to play with them. As a result, I spent the early years of my life being horribly ill.

When I was in my 30s I learned I had no immunity to rubella. The hospital I worked at required me to be inoculated. I was told Childhood immunity isn't always permanent, especially if you were very young when you first had the measles. I had had the measles three times before I was 10.

I lost my hearing after running a temperature of 110. Mom had said high temperatures were normal for little kids. She packed me in ice, rubbed me down with iced alcohol and gave me lots of children's aspirin. Not once did she consider bringing me to the hospital.

I also suffered constant ear infections. Ear infections my pediatrician said were caused by cigarette smoke. My Mom and Dad and Grandparents and Uncles and Aunts ALL smoked. The idea that something so universally accepted (in those days) could cause ear problems seemed outrageous to my Mom. So everyone continued to smoke in the house.

Mom told me the infections were caused by water in my ear. She told me I had to be careful when I washed my hair or went swimming. She told me to ALWAYS dry my ears out with a Q-tip the moment I got out of a pool or the tub. The infections continued.

Growing up I was sick much of the time. Much of these illnesses were preventable. I wonder what my current health would be like, had I my Mom given proper care?

☙Epilogue

I remember the morning my mother died. It's frozen in my mind, locked there forever. I can still feel the crisp chill lingering in the air, the sound of birds chattering in my yard, and the smell of jasmine wafting in through the back door.

Mom died, and suddenly I was alone. Free. But I'd forgotten who I was. I was ill, beaten down, tired beyond words and lost. Five years had gone by since my father passed on, and my brother left the state. Five years when the biggest part of me was left to die alone, inch by inch, forgotten and cast aside.

When Mom died, those five years were suddenly wrapped up inside a single moment and suspended in time. Five years of indefinable emotion, something akin to longing, pain, and loss … too intense to be spoken, too horrific to be felt, and much too much to be understood.

I never felt as if I had a choice. So I gave my life away. Sacrificed my health, my youth, my future, for a chance at getting love, from someone so wounded she was incapable of giving it. So I set aside my pain to ease hers, ignored my needs so I could see to hers, and became what I thought she needed me to be.

Somehow over the years I forgot who I was and everything I ever hoped to be. Then I tried to bury all feeling deep within my soul and forget what being "me" felt like.

Nowadays I dream. In dreams my Mother is everything a Good Mother should be. In dreams I receive unconditional and healing love. In dreams there is no abuse, no neglect, and no illness. In dreams I grow up feeling safe and warm and loved.

In dreams "rape" is a seed planted by farmers. In dreams the hot sun doesn't burn my skin, the 3pm sky is blue, NOT white as steam, and I do not melt away or vanish. My family is still alive and I am NOT alone. I am whole and healthy and all is well with the world.

In dreams I'm free and never long for death again.

My God grant us all blessings and ONLY sweet dreams.

The sky as seen from our backyard ~ August of 2007

www.ingramcontent.com/pod-product-compliance
Lightning Source LLC
Chambersburg PA
CBHW081100290526
45795CB00006B/1941

* 9 7 8 1 4 9 2 3 0 0 4 9 6 *